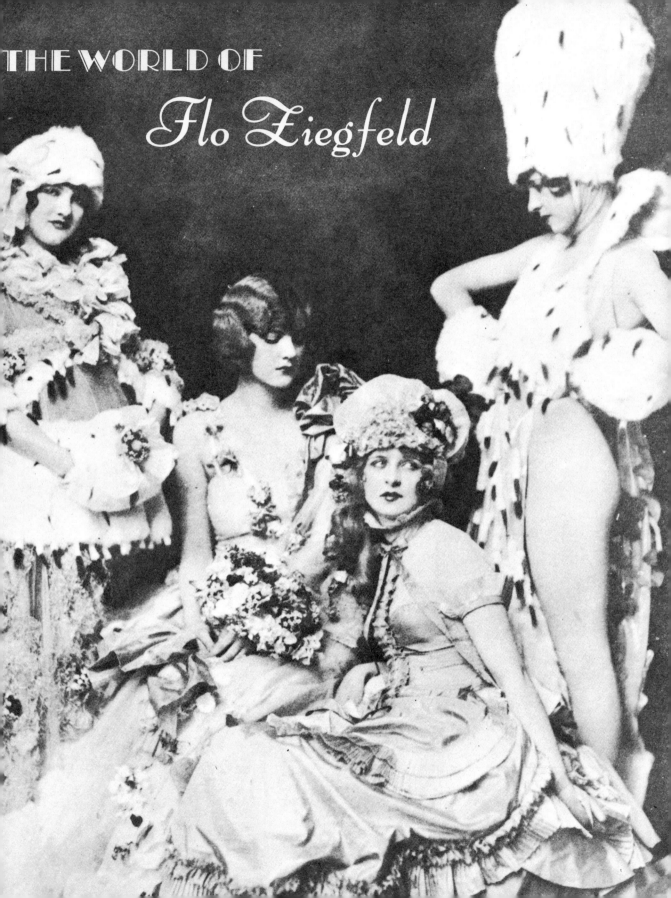

THE WORLD OF
Flo Ziegfeld

THE WORLD OF

Flo Ziegfeld

RANDOLPH CARTER

Praeger Publishers

NEW YORK · WASHINGTON

Published in the United States of America in 1974
by Praeger Publishers, Inc.
111 Fourth Avenue, New York, N.Y. 10003

Library of Congress Cataloging in Publication Data

Carter, Randolph.
The world of Flo Ziegfeld.

1. Ziegfeld, Florenz, 1869–1932.   I. Title.
PN2287.Z5C34   792.0232 0924 [B]   74–3065
ISBN 0–275–19990–6

This book was originated
and edited by Christine Bernard
and Charles Spencer

Designed and produced by Paul Elek Ltd, London

Printed in Great Britain

The illustration on the first page of
the book and on the back of the
jacket shows a group of girls
from the *Follies* in John Harkrider
costumes. The photo is by
Ziegfeld's photographer-in-chief,
Alfred Cheney Johnston

FRONTISPIECE: Flo Ziegfeld Jnr,
aged about twenty-eight

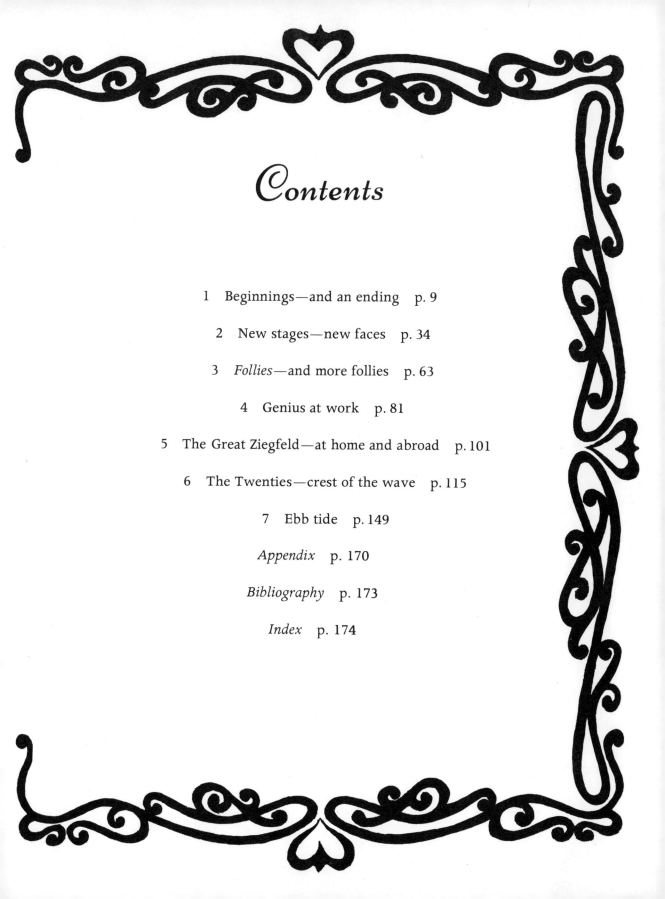

Contents

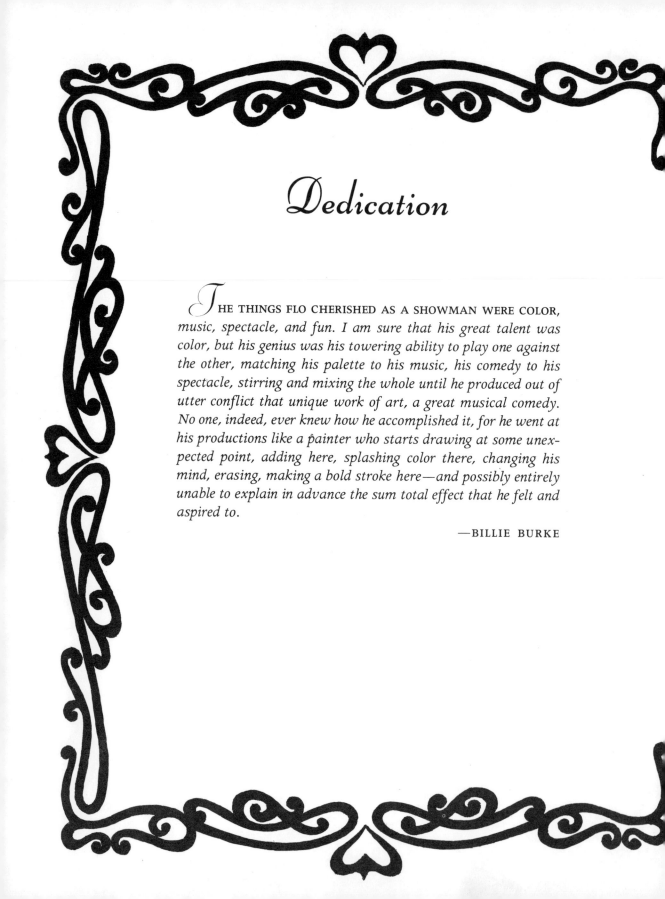

Dedication

THE THINGS FLO CHERISHED AS A SHOWMAN WERE COLOR, *music, spectacle, and fun. I am sure that his great talent was color, but his genius was his towering ability to play one against the other, matching his palette to his music, his comedy to his spectacle, stirring and mixing the whole until he produced out of utter conflict that unique work of art, a great musical comedy. No one, indeed, ever knew how he accomplished it, for he went at his productions like a painter who starts drawing at some unexpected point, adding here, splashing color there, changing his mind, erasing, making a bold stroke here—and possibly entirely unable to explain in advance the sum total effect that he felt and aspired to.*

—BILLIE BURKE

Acknowledgements

I AM DEEPLY GRATEFUL TO THE MANY WHO HAVE ASSISTED me in research and preparation of the manuscript, to Gretl Urban, Patricia Ziegfeld Stephenson, Lillian Gish, Paula Trueman, Alan Brock, Helen Bolstad, Martin Battersby, and to Doris Vinton of the Ziegfeld Club. Dr. Roderick Bladel, Maxwell Silverman, Donald Fowle, Dorothy Swerdlove and the entire staff of the Theatre Collection of the New York Public Library at Lincoln Center have been unfailingly courteous and helpful. I owe a special debt of gratitude to Bernard Crystal of the Department of Special Collections, Columbia University, for allowing me unrestricted access to the Urban Collection. Robert Heide and John Gillman, Romano Tozzi, Ron Link and Jerry Glover have all been generous in contributing photographs and prints from their respective collections. David Loffert, who has worked closely with me since the book's inception, is responsible for much of the photographic work, but my thanks are also due to Larry McBrearty and Beverly Kalehoff for their expert assistance in that department. Christine Bernard has been a most sympathetic and perceptive editor while Eugene Sorensen has patiently and impatiently typed and retyped the manuscript. Finally thanks are due to Charles Spencer and John Cromwell who bear initial responsibility for the enterprise.

1
Beginnings
and
an Ending

PROFESSIONAL ASTROLOGERS, IN STRESSING THE POWER OF the Cardinal Sign of Aries, have frequently pointed to Florenz Ziegfeld Jr. as an example of one born at that auspicious time. The date: 21 March 1868. Unfortunately, the precise moment of arrival is not a matter of record, but it must have occurred at an instant of climactic conjunction of heavenly bodies. Initiative, originality, action and leadership are key words for Aries, but Florenz Jr. was also amply endowed with daring, daring bordering on the reckless, imagination, charm (when he cared to exert it), talent and an ability to head straight for a goal even by uncharted paths.

These endowments were not immediately evident to his father, Dr. Florenz Ziegfeld, President of the Chicago Musical College which he himself had founded in 1867, and whom his contemporary, George Ade Davis, hailed as 'one of the most picturesque figures in the History of Musical Development in

Urban's study for his Ziegfeld Theatre; it was built in 1926

America, a pioneer who has lived to see the successful combination of his labors, to watch the growth, the budding and the blossoming of musical development and even see the matured and ripened fruit as well. His autograph across the pages of musical history of the Western World will never be defaced.'

As a son of so illustrious a sire, Florenz Jr. was a distinct disappointment. Frail, lethargic and apathetic to music, which he studied under compulsion, he showed very little zest for anything until the age of seventeen when his parents, in desperation, dispatched him to a cattle ranch in Wyoming. Freed of Teutonic restraints his natural ebullience soared alarmingly. When he returned some months later he had not only developed a will of his own but had become sufficiently expert with a six-shooter to join Buffalo Bill's Wild West Show. Dr. Ziegfeld soon put an end to that engagement, but it marked the beginning of the career of one of America's greatest showmen. Dr. Ziegfeld's signature is somewhat blurred, but Florenz Ziegfeld Jr. has left his mark on the musical theatre, not only in America but throughout the world, on styles, design, production techniques, music, dance and finally motion pictures.

His first steps were not particularly rewarding and undoubtedly caused Dr. Ziegfeld further pain, but they did display the extravagance and flair for publicity which was to characterize his later career. The directors of the Columbian Exposition, Chicago's World Fair, had assigned Dr. Ziegfeld the task of providing musical entertainment to be presented in the enormous First Regiment Armory, rebuilt and rechristened The Trocadero. Young Ziegfeld somehow induced his father to allow him to act as impresario, whereupon he took off to Europe in the fall of 1892, and returned with seven leading musical ensembles including the Von Bühlow Military Band of Hamburg, the Voros Miska Band of Hungary, a large and expensive collection of French and Russian artists and an eccentric English dancer, Maggie Potts, alluringly billed 'Cyrene.' The show was a disastrous failure. Undaunted, Ziegfeld journeyed to New York where The Great Sandow, an amiable twenty-three year old muscleman, was enjoying only moderate success at the Casino, in spite of the fact that his

Dr Florenz Ziegfeld, President of the Chicago Musical College, in 1882

Flo with his brother and sister

10

abdominal muscles, when tensed, were said to 'produce a wonderful checkerboard arrangement of fibres, the existence of which modern anatomists deny, though plainly visible at a distance of thirty feet.'

The Great Sandow really had a great act. He first appeared in silk trunks and struck a series of Classical Art Poses. These were followed by an exhibition of chest expansion (4′ 10″) after which he juggled a man and allowed him to sit on the palm of his hand. He raised a huge dumbell which, when lowered, revealed a man concealed in each ball. He then lifted a grand piano with a group of men seated upon it. When Sandow finally lay down for a rest, a plank was placed across his chest and three horses walked across it.

When Sandow opened at the Trocadero in August, 1893, he proved very much to Chicago's taste, especially as exploited by Ziegfeld, who, without undue persuasion, induced Mrs. Potter Palmer, a monument of social prominence, to journey backstage personally to inspect Sandow's muscles. 'What wonderful muscles you have, Mr. Sandow!' she observed.

'Feel them,' suggested Sandow.

Mrs. Palmer ran her fingers over the corrugated surface of his massive chest and later confessed to having been 'thrilled to the spine.'

This observation led to a flock of prominent men and women making backstage visits to feel Sandow's muscles and to marvel at such strength and beauty. Weekly grosses at the Trocadero jumped from two thousand dollars to twenty-eight thousand dollars, and The Great Sandow, who had agreed to a percentage deal, found himself making an unbelievable three thousand dollars per week.

After the fair closed, Sandow made a couple of national tours under Ziegfeld's aegis and became something of a national figure. The end came, however, at San Francisco's Mid-Winter Fair. At Boon's Arena, a proposed fight between a lion and a bear had aroused the entire Pacific Coast. Columns in the California press were devoted to editorials denouncing the match while the sporting pages were filled with discussions of the respective prowess of the two beasts. Seats were selling at fifty dollars apiece on the night of the encounter, but before the animals could face one another, the police intervened and

American poster, c. 1885
Huntington Hartford Collection

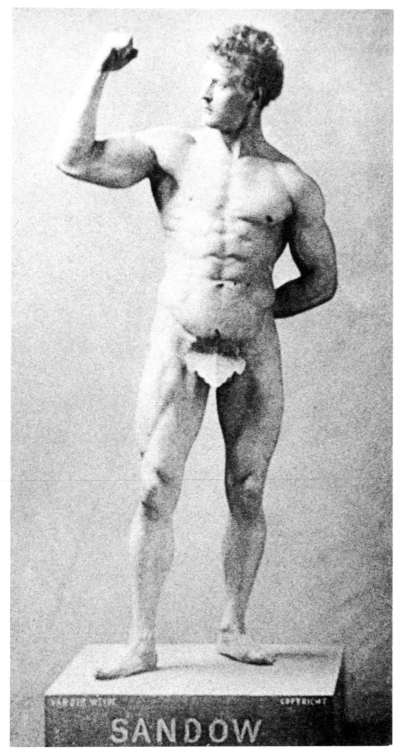

12

Two American theatre posters.
N.Y. Gallery of Modern Art

the performance was canceled.

Ziegfeld immediately saw his opportunity and grasped it. In the newspapers the following morning, he challenged the owner of the lion to a fight between the animal and Sandow. The challenge was accepted, and the match aroused such excitement that Ziegfeld was forced to erect a huge circus tent with a capacity of ten thousand. The night of the contest it was full to overflowing. Unfortunately, there are several versions of the incident; one is told with considerable relish by William A. Brady, himself an ardent sportsman and hunter. According to Brady, the lion had been so mercilessly clubbed at 'rehearsals,' including a series of blows on the nose, that at the sight of Sandow he simply rolled over. In any event, from the points of view of both the lion and Sandow, the contest was a distinct defeat, though certainly Flo and Sandow received their share of the eighteen thousand dollars take.

Though Anna Held was one of the most widely publicized women of her day, a certain air of mystery, always seems to hover about her. Of obscure origins, the daughter of Polish-Jewish parents, she was born in Paris about 1873. In dazzling, disjointed interviews she would tell of toiling as a child cleaning and curling plumes ('I knew I should one day be wearing them'), stitching fur caps, and finally at the age of eight, singing for *sous* on the streets of Montmartre. Orphaned at twelve and finding herself in London, she managed to secure a job in the chorus line at the Prince's Theatre at five shillings a week. But Anna was not destined for any chorus line. After a solo appearance in an Amsterdam Music hall, engagements in cabarets in Scandinavia, Germany and Hungary followed; at fifteen she was already featured in revues at *El Dorado* and *La Scala* in Paris, both precursors of the *Folies-Bergères*.

Anna Held's talent may have been minor, but her intimate style, her studied artifice, her tiny exquisite body, fascinated audiences, especially when she sang 'Won't You Come and Play With Me?', a song adapted from *Die Kleine Schrecke* ('The Little Teaser') which she had sung at the Wintergarden in Berlin and which eventually became her trademark:

Won't you come and play wiz me
As I have such a nice little way wiz me . . .

Two studio portraits of the great Sandow, *c.* 1884. *New York Public Library*

13

An early photo of Anna Held,
c. 1890, before she met Ziegfeld

When in the late Spring of 1896 Ziegfeld saw Anna Held at the
Palace Theatre in London, he knew he had at last discovered
a worthy successor to The Great Sandow. He had also found
a mistress whose flair and extravagance was a match for his
own. Somewhere in transit, Anna had married Maximo
Carrera, a shadowy South American figure who appeared
willing to fade completely into the background, leaving only
a brooding daughter, Liane, whom Anna discreetly placed in
a French convent. Word was given out to the newspapers that
Anna and Ziegfeld had been married in Paris, although in fact
no marriage ever took place, a fact which was not revealed
until some fifteen years later, when she was recognized as his
'common law' wife.

The Great White Way up which Anna and Flo presently
moved with such *élan* was quite different from the rather
barren landscape of Broadway today. Though lacking in the
luster Ziegfeld was later to impart to it, Broadway consisted of

14

a glittering band of some forty theatres, many spilling over into the side streets, stretching from Twenty-Third Street to Mr. Charles Frohman's splendid new Empire Theatre at Fortieth Street, and encompassing such famous playhouses as Palmers, Wallachs, Weber and Fields Music Hall, Hammersteins, the Knickerbocker and the Metropolitan Opera. A rich assortment of Lobster Palaces and such restaurants as Murray's, an elaborate Egyptian establishment, glowed between the blazing marquees to form a dazzling backdrop for the fashionable throngs.

Rectors, between Forty-Third and Forty-Fourth Streets on Longacre Square (not yet christened Times Square which occurred with the advent of the Times Tower) was the supreme after-theatre shrine. 'I found Broadway a quiet little lane of ham and eggs and left it a full blown avenue of lobsters and champagne,' declared Charles Rector, whose career began as the driver of a horsecar on Second Avenue.

15

WAS THERE EVER A PAL
LIKE YOU

by
Irving Berlin

Billie Burke

Irving Berlin, Inc.
Music Publishers
1587 Broadway
New York

Price 60¢

Decorated in green and gold in the Louis XIV style and lighted by crystal chandeliers reflected in ceiling-high mirrors, the establishment, sometimes referred to as 'The Court of Triviality' and 'The Cathedral of Froth,' contained one hundred tables downstairs, seventy-five upstairs, four private dining rooms and the first revolving door ever seen in New York. Through this door—the real summit of the Great White Way—passed the élite into 'the centre of the web spun by the benevolent spider of Manhattan in its quest to snare the genius, ability and beauty of America,' an apt phrase said to have been coined by Diamond Jim Brady.

A contemporary account describes Anna Held's entrance: 'Poised, while a gypsy violinist established himself at the train of her dress, Miss Anna Held swept into the room—the violinist serenading her softly—a vision in yellow crêpe de chine trimmed with poppies in full bloom, her wide open eyes an open invitation to French Frivolity.' Ziegfeld had just presented her in *Papa's Wife*, in which trifle she had enchanted audiences with the song, 'I Just Can't Make My Eyes Behave.' Ziegfeld on that occasion was described as 'tall, somewhat stooped and saturnine.'

Papa's Wife marked Anna's second appearance in New York and the first under the Ziegfeld banner. Her debut had been a brief but brilliantly spotted apparition, an alluring ghost in Evans and Hoey's revival of Charles Hoyt's, *A Parlor Match*, which prompted the *New York Times* to observe: 'As a spectacle Mlle. Held is a success, absolute and complete. Her eyes are long, narrow and heavily circled; her nose is straight; her mouth perfect; and as for her chin, people might go some ways to see it without regretting the experience.' Of her abilities there were reservations. 'Her voice is not sweet or very strong . . . She would not be a "sensation" at all if the idea had not been ingeniously forced on the public that she is—naughty.'

Anna was a willing accomplice in Ziegfeld's quest for headlines. Automobile racing was all the rage. She publicly challenged any American woman to race her from New York to Philadelphia, but warned that she held a couple of European speed records, had driven ninety miles in 193 minutes and had once actually covered three and a half miles in five minutes.

19

The challenge was never met, due possibly to these alarming statistics. On another occasion every newspaper in New York received information through regular news channels that Miss Held, while riding her bicycle along the causeway, had stopped a runaway horse and saved a well-known city magistrate from serious injury, possibly even death. All the papers printed glowing accounts of Miss Held's bravery and *The Herald* actually devoted two columns to her exploit, accompanied by a sketch of the heroine on her bike. But the stunt which really put Anna over and made her name a household word was Ziegfeld's brilliant notion of having forty gallons of milk delivered from New Jersey every day to their suite at the Netherland. It was announced that the milk was for Miss Held's bath. When the newspapers were sceptical, Ziegfeld escorted a delegation of reporters to view Miss Held immersed in milk. 'It is, you see, to take zee beauty bath,' she explained. 'In Paris I ate some fish and it brought out a peemple on my wrist. The milk she preserve zee creamy complexion.' The story rocked two continents and to keep it going, Ziegfeld arranged to have the dairyman sue him for non-payment, his defense being that the milk was sour. A forgotten French beauty announced that she had been bathing in ass's milk for some time, that she had communicated this intelligence to the Paris *Figaro* and that Ziegfeld had got the idea from her (which he had); she threatened to sue. Ziegfeld countered, claiming historical precedent, citing the fact that certain beauties of the French court frequently bathed in milk which was surreptitiously resold. In its Sunday supplement *The World* ran a picture of the Queen of Madagascar receiving callers in her tub, her dusky body rising out of what certainly appeared to be milk. Women of fashion everywhere began bathing, or at least sponge bathing in milk, and Anna Held's baths became a legend which still clings to her name.

Ziegfeld's shows for Anna were tailor-made: *Papa's Wife, The French Maid, The Parisian Model, Little Duchess, Mlle. Napolean, Miss Innocence,* all included elaborate dance numbers, both ballet and precision, a sketch of a plot, lots of girls—Anna was not afraid of competition—the star sumptuously gowned, rolling her eyes, lifting her skirts and concluding the evening with 'Won't You Come and Play Wiz Me?' 'A

Anna Held

RIGHT: Anna Held in 1906.
Author's collection

20

nymphic Anna pitted her beauty against a dozen others,' wrote a dazzled critic. 'Most stars balk at too radiantly lovely opposition, but not Anna. The Milk has not curdled in her baths.'

Anna's shows were considered outrageously naughty, and when she toured, the whole nation was alerted. *The Pittsburgh Post* sounded a typical alarm:

> Police censorship has caused the removal of portraits of Anna Held from the lobby of the Nixon Theatre. The piece which Inspector McQuade especially frowned on was in a frame almost six feet square and showed a scene in an artistic studio in the second act of *The Parisian Model*. The police refused to countenance the exhibition of her bare shoulders and feet in the theatre lobby and there is speculation and fear as to what will happen to the production when it comes here next week.

During the run of *Miss Innocence*, one of Anna's most elaborate and successful extravaganzas (one of the gowns designed by Pascaud of Paris was encrusted with diamonds and was said to have cost untold thousands) Ziegfeld announced Anna's retirement which caused considerable consternation and prompted some rather caustic comment in certain quarters. *The New York Review* of 28 November 1909 observed:

GOODBYE FLO!

Flo Ziegfeld is now advertizing that Anna Held is on her farewell tour. Is Ziegfeld going to let his meal ticket get away from him? The 'farewell tour' dodge has become so discredited it is astonishing that even Ziegfeld would resort to that threadbare device. Will Miss Held retire? Not if he can help it. It was Miss Held's name that procured him credit. Because of his alliance with her [a typical reference to their marital status] he was permitted to gamble 'in memo', running up debts at the roulette wheel that he subsequently repudiated by stopping payment on the check given in settlement. With Anna Held out of the field he probably never would have another opportunity to proclaim himself 'welcher' as he did in a recent suit brought by the proprietor of a gambling house to collect the money Ziegfeld lost.

When Anna toured, her private railroad car, decorated in Oriental style, contained potted palms, sumptuous furnishings and even a grand piano. A five-piece band accompanied her

TOP: Anna Held in the first
Ziegfeld Follies of 1907

wherever she went. Frequent European jaunts with Flo were no less lavish. She turned up at Biarritz in a sable coat made from a hundred and ten choice pelts; at the *Fête des Fleurs* in Paris she won first prize in an orchid-bedecked four-in-hand carriage. After cheerfully gambling away thousands at Monte Carlo, the Ziegfelds might arrive triumphantly at the Lido accompanied by Sandow and Lillian Russell, or at some other fashionable spa escorted by a glittering entourage.

Back in 1896 seven powerful theatre owners, Mark Klaw, Abraham Lincoln Erlanger, Charles Frohman and his brother Daniel, Sam Nixon, Abe Hayman and J. F. Zimmerman sat down to lunch in New York's most fashionable hotel, the Holland House. (Klaw, in spite of his rather alarming name, was not particularly menacing. He is best remembered for his opinion of first-nighters: 'Theatre habitués and sons of habitués.' Abe Erlanger is better forgotten. In his day he was the most ruthless and hated man in the theatre. Charles Frohman, a personage of considerable taste and talent, was known both as 'Mr. Theater' and 'The Star Maker.') The burden of their talk concerned the general disorder of booking practices in New York and more especially on the far flung Road. By the time lunch was over, they had founded a trust to be set up in New York with a central booking office, an efficient system which they hoped would bring order to the prevailing chaos. This syndicate, under the direction of Klaw and Erlanger, and largely due to the efforts of 'dishonest Abe', as Erlanger came to be known, succeeded beyond all expectations.

By consolidating their extensive holdings, and systematically absorbing smaller operators, they were not long in welding a nationwide chain which amounted to virtual monopoly. Theatre owners who failed to knuckle under to the power of the Syndicate were denied bookings, and producers who failed to meet outrageous terms were excluded from theatres. For a time such famous actor-managers as James Jefferson, James O'Neill, Nat Goodwin, Richard Mansfield and Minnie Maddern Fiske fought back, but only Mrs. Fiske, probably America's finest actress, held out, with the result

LEFT: Anna Held in 1906.
Author's collection

23

that she spent the balance of her career playing in small towns and drafty gymnasiums. Even Sarah Bernhardt was forced into circus tents.

Abe Erlanger, not insensitive to the hatred he inspired, eventually ordered a stongly re-inforced, foot-thick door to his grubby office on Forty-Second Street and trembled when the barber came to shave his heavy jowls. His real nemesis, however, came out of Syracuse, New York, in the form of the Brothers Shubert, (née Semanski) Sam, Lee and J. J. (Jake) who, with Machiavellian manoeuvres even Abe could not counter, eventually smashed the Syndicate to form an empire of their own which was to dominate the American theatre until 1956 when the Shubert monopoly was broken by government decree. J. J. Shubert then made a statement which, though tempered, had the ring of truth and was certainly prophetic:

> The decree requires us to sell a number of theatres which were assembled over half a century. Whether these theatres in other hands will continue to be operated as legitimate houses only time will tell. As the last survivor of the three Shubert brothers who practically alone developed the present theatrical districts in the larger cities of the United States, I can point out what my brothers and I contributed to the development of the legitimate theatre in America. I will live up to the decree, although I have my doubts as to whether some of its provisions will not hurt rather than benefit the legitimate theatre.

Sarah Bernhardt photographed on a visit to the United States

Charles Frohman, known as 'Mr Theatre'; with colleagues he formed a Syndicate which became a nationwide monopoly and forced many non-cooperators out of business

Even the great Sarah was forced by the Syndicate to perform in a circus tent in June 1906. Nothing daunted, she carried the Texas audience by storm

There was always something distinctly alarming about J. J.'s rages, especially if one happened to be the object of his fury. His ferret eyes would shift dangerously, his portly body contract, squid-like, a terrible moment of trembling, then explosive, poisonous blasts would darken the air, frequently spelling doom even to innocent bystanders. The very mention of Ziegfeld's name, years after his death, could trigger harsh vibrations, compounded in memory, generated by envy and pique to cause J. J. to exclaim majestically: 'You know and I know I'm unforgiveable.'

The friction between Ziegfeld and the Shuberts began in 1906, at the time the Shuberts were forming their Independent Circuit. Needing attractions quite as much as theatres, the Shuberts looked with covetous eyes upon Anna Held who was then in Paris with Ziegfeld. At the same time Klaw and Erlanger were becoming interested in Miss Held's future, and it wasn't long before both factions were bidding for the privilege of presenting her in their respective theatres.

25

The Ziegfelds did indeed return to America but Ziegfeld immediately arranged with Klaw and Erlanger to star his wife in *The Parisian Model*. The Shuberts were deeply pained over the outcome of their contribution to the Ziegfelds' travelling expenses. Lee wrote:

to ZIEGFELD

WILL CABLE YOU $1,000 FOR SAILING PURPOSE. ANSWER.
                                                    LEE SHUBERT

to SHUBERT

PERSONAL INTERVIEW IMPERATIVE: MY CABLE STATED ONLY TERMS UNDER WHICH I WOULD SAIL AT ONCE. ANSWER TODAY OR TOO LATE.
                                                    ZIEGFELD

to ZIEGFELD

CASINO OPENS SPRING: PLAY 'MOTOR GIRL' GREAT STAR PART. SALARY HELD $1,000 FIFTY PERCENT PROFITS I MAKE PRODUCTION. WILL SEND YOU THOUSAND ON CONDITION THAT MADAME HELD SEND CABLE. ORIGINAL OF WHICH SHE MUST SIGN, STATING THAT IF WE SHOULD BE UNABLE TO AGREE ON A CO-PARTNERSHIP THAT SHE WILL AGREE THAT HER FIRST TOUR OF THIS COUNTRY IMMEDIATELY UPON HER RETURN MUST BE IN THEATRES OR OPERA HOUSES BOOKED OR CONTROLLED BY US.
                                                    LEE SHUBERT

The Ziegfelds had completed another tour of Continental casinos and were, thanks to Ziegfeld's passion for gambling, practically penniless. In March 1906 the following exchange of telegrams occurred:

My Dear Ziegfeld:
You having failed to make a contract between ourselves and Miss Anna Held in accordance with the terms of the cables which have passed between us, I hereby demand of you immediately the return of the sum of $1,000 advanced to you and which said sum you agreed to return, providing you failed to deliver to us a contract with Miss Held.

Yours truly
Lee Shubert

On the advice of Klaw and Erlanger whose lawyers cited legal technicalities, Ziegfeld refused to return the money and the Shubert Theatrical Company instituted court action. The case dragged on for several seasons. A judgment was finally settled in favor of the Shuberts, but the Shuberts, who had long memories, never forgot. Ziegfeld, due to his extravagance and lack of business acumen, was undoubtedly the architect of his own destruction, but the Shuberts were ever present to lend a helping hand. In any event, no Ziegfeld production was ever presented in a Shubert house.

Lee Shubert, a life-long enemy of Flo's

BEAUTIFUL WOMEN OF THE STAGE

Contemporary ornamental design.

LEFT: The young Mae West – one of the few American stars of the day to withstand Flo's attempts to lure her into the *Follies*

'Your American girls are so beautiful', Anna is reported to have remarked; 'The most beautiful girls in the world. If you could dress them up *chic*, you'd have a better show than the *Folies-Bergère*.' Ziegfeld, who had been eyeing the *Folies-Bergère* for some time, acted on her advice. It was Anna Held who proposed the title *Follies* to Ziegfeld, not, as is generally assumed, in imitation of the *Folies-Bergère* but basing it on a New York newspaper column *Follies of the Day*. She suggested an adaptation, *Follies of the Year*, but Ziegfeld superstitiously insisted on the title containing exactly thirteen letters—hence

27

Follies of 1907. As this title suggests, the shows were originally framed around a series of humorous comments on the events of the year, but once beautiful girls and spectacle took over the comedians were largely edged out.

With Klaw and Erlanger footing the bill to the tune of thirteen thousand dollars for scenery and costumes, and three thousand eight hundred dollars in salaries and overhead, (Ziegfeld was paid two hundred dollars a week) the first *Follies* opened in the 'Jardin de Paris,' the roof garden of the New York Theatre, in July, 1907. It had a chorus line of fifty beauties billed as 'The Anna Held Girls,' but Anna wasn't in it. Annabelle Whitford held the spotlight as The Gibson Bathing Girl in stockings and bloomers. Mlle. Dazie did the Ju-Jitsu Waltz with Prince Tokio—'straight from Japan'—and also appeared as Salome. Prima Donna Grace La Rue sang 'Miss Ginger From Jamaica' and comedian Dave Lewis introduced the novelty song, 'I Oughtn't To Auto Anymore.' The big production number had the entire chorus marching up and down the aisles whipping snare drums. People were shocked

Bert Lahr (*centre*) in vaudeville, 1907: he later starred in the Ziegfeld *Follies*

RIGHT: 'Shine on Harvest Moon' – Nora Bayes' great show-stopper – was rapturously received both in 1908 and when sung by Ruth Etting in the last *Follies* of all in 1931. *Heide Gillman Collection*

28

by Annabelle's bloomers and the show's general raciness. As one critic observed:

> In seeking to reproduce some of the audacities of the French capital, Mr. Ziegfeld has come occasionally into collusion with a sense of propriety which still distinguishes a large portion of the public over here. But the action of the *Follies* is so fast that a state of delirious acquiescence is induced. The auditor resigns himself to fate, and at the conclusion of the performance departs, like a passenger on one of those switch-back devices which provide thrills at summer resorts, conscious that he has been scared now and then, but not irreparably shocked and tempted to try it again.

After runs in Washington and Baltimore, the production ended up with a profit of $120,000.

In the 1908 edition the *Follies* moved to Erlanger's New York Theatre. Ziegfeld's name went up in lights for the first time. He also had his first song hit when Nora Bayes and her husband, Jack Norworth, introduced 'Shine On Harvest Moon' which they had also written. Mae Murray appeared as the Nell Brinkley Girl, the popular cover girl of the day, and Lucy Weston, the naughty-but-nice English singer who specialized in the *double-entendre*, made a big hit with 'As You Walk Down the Strand'. Even more detailed attention was given to the Girls who were featured in 'Take Me Around In A Taxicab' in which they paraded with taxi meters attached to their shoulder flicking 'ON' and 'OFF'. The show ran 120 performances.

The *Ziegfeld Follies of 1909* (Flo now decided to make the *Follies* an annual event) was even more elaborate and successful. One spectacular scene had the girls wearing hats representing warships. When the house lights darkened, their headgear lighted up with searching spotlights and blazing portholes and the entire U.S. Fleet passed in review. Even more spectacular was the appearance of Lillian Lorraine who dazzled both audiences and Flo in 'Up, Up, Up, In My Aeroplane', circling above the patrons in a miniature flying machine and scattering roses.

As photographs attest, Lillian Lorraine was truly dazzling. Ziegfeld dubbed her The Most Beautiful Woman In the World. She dazzled on stage and off in diamonds and floor-length

ermine wraps. Her audacious bathing suits were the scandal of Long Beach and she wore the first ankle bracelet ever displayed on Broadway. During her association with Ziegfeld her career bordered on the manic, a crush of parties, publicity, jewels and scandal. In a quarrel over her favors, Frank Harwood of the New York Harwoods shot and killed aeronaut Tony van Pühl. She married, divorced, remarried and divorced Frederic Gresheimer, son of a wealthy department store owner, sold her jewels estimated at one hundred thousand dollars and was in and out of bankruptcy. Smoking while drunk, she set fire to her room in a boarding house and was rushed to Bellevue unconscious. She injured her spine in a fall on an icy pavement and the newspapers labelled her, 'Broken Butterfly.' In 1933, after Ziegfeld's death, when the Ziegfeld Theatre was re-opened as a motion picture house, Lillian, as a guest celebrity, was asked to sing her old song, 'By The Light Of The Silvery Moon.' Gus Edwards at the piano played the opening chords, but when Lillian opened her mouth to sing no sound came out. Tears ran down her cheeks and she had to be escorted back to her seat in the audience.

Billie Burke, who was certainly closer to Ziegfeld than anyone—even Anna—wrote in her memoirs, 'Of all the girls in Flo's life I think I was most jealous of Lillian. I think he really loved her.' Flo's obsessive passion for Lillian, publicly flaunted (Flo even installed Lillian in a suite in The Ansonia, the same hotel in which he and Anna shared apartments) was bitterly humiliating to Anna. Rumors and even details of the break-up of their marriage were thoroughly aired in the gossip columns. Anna described her husband at breakfast as 'buried in newspapers. If he would only say something—if he would even say, Damn!' From Paris she announced, during one of her frequent visits, 'If Mr. Ziegfeld wants to see me he can come here. I have worked very hard. I need a rest. I love Paris, but I do not enjoy going about without my husband.' Flo announced that he would love to join her in Paris but was 'too busy'. In 1912 Anna finally sued for divorce, and for the first time the marital status of Anna and Flo was discussed in the public press. *The Courier* of 7 August 1912 carried the following item:

It was announced today that when Miss Anna Held appeared

Members of the public picking over the personal effects of Anna Held at the Waldorf-Astoria, after her death in 1918

LEFT: Dubbed 'the most beautiful woman in the world' in 1915, Lillian Lorraine was star of the *Follies. N.Y. Public Library*

'Of all the girls in Flo's life, I was most jealous of Lillian.' Billie Burke of Lillian Lorraine

before Edward G. Whitaker as referee in her suit for divorce against Florenz Ziegfeld, she testified that no ceremony had ever taken place. Miss Held testified that in the presence of other persons she and Mr. Ziegfeld accepted each other as husband and wife. In reply to questions from the referee, Miss Held said that she had ever since held herself to be the wife of Ziegfeld and that he had publicly declared himself to be her husband. Miss Held's first husband, Maximo Carrera, being deceased, the referee declared her marriage to Florenz Ziegfeld Jr. legal by common law.

Five years later when Anna was dying, Flo, then married to Billie Burke, asked Billie: 'Will you send her something?'

Billie replied that she would. In her memoirs she wrote: 'I

Anna Held with her daughter Liane

was glad to. I sent her fresh eggs, baby broilers, fresh veg-
etables and butter daily, and my own doctor. But it was too
late.'

Anna asked for Ziegfeld before she died, but he never came.
It was a slow, rather agonizing death caused by a bone
infection, excessive dieting and overwork. (She collapsed after
a nation-wide tour in *Follow Me* for the Shuberts.) The
obituaries were fulsome and even slightly ghoulish, diagnos-
ing her death as 'myeloma', stressing the tight lacing of her
corsets and the fact that she weighed less than seventy

32

pounds. Flo sent a magnificent blanket of orchids to be placed on her coffin, but he did not attend the funeral. As the cortege left Campbell's Funeral Church, some five thousand people jammed the pavements along Broadway.

Under the press picture reproduced on p. 31 of people picking over her effects was the caption: 'Jewels, costumes and personal effects of the late Anna Held were placed on sale at the Waldorf-Astoria by the attorney of the dead actress. Her estate has been estimated at quarter of a million dollars; a great part in jewels and works of art. The proceeds of the sale will be held in trust for Anna Held's daughter, Liane Carrera, until she is twenty-five.'

Liane, who always despised Ziegfeld and never ceased to accuse him of cruelty and neglect, had grown very close to her mother after the divorce. Against Anna's better judgment she even made an attempt to follow in her mother's footsteps. Of her debut in Brooklyn, the *Brooklyn Eagle* commented: 'Apparently there was much activity in getting Liane Carrera ready for the stage. . . . She was assisted by six extremely healthy young women. She is well meaning, but disappointing. Her French lisp is appealing, but natural roguishness is missing. Liane's eyes are serious.' She tried again after her mother's death under the name of Anna Held Jr.

In the early thirties Liane Carrera operated a bar and restaurant in the East Fifties near Beekman Place called, *Anna Held's Town Club*. It was dominated by a large painting of Anna, but in spite of the patronage of such current celebrities as Claudia Morgan, Alexander Kirkland, Zita Johann and Sidney Kingsley, it never really caught on.

In 1954 a volume of memoirs purportedly by Anna entitled, *Une Etoile Française ou Ciel de l'Amèrique,* was published in Paris. Never translated, it recounts some fairly lurid episodes concerning a jewel robbery engineered by Flo and a savage abortion performed on the dining-room table by 'a seedy-looking doctor who smelled of alcohol', assisted by Ziegfeld. Liane Carrera emerges as a figure of considerable nobility, and even triumphs on stage when she heroically steps into her mother's shoes and brings an audience to its feet. In minuscule print appears the line: 'Copyright, 1954, by Liane Carrera.'

Liane Carrera was tempted to follow in her mother's footsteps – but had little success. *N.Y. Public Library*

2
New Stages—
New Faces

WHEN ABE ERLANGER'S NEW AMSTERDAM THEATRE OPENED on 4 September 1906, *The New York Times* rhapsodized:

THE HOUSE BEAUTIFUL

In the New Amsterdam, Art Nouveau, first crystallized in the Paris Exposition of 1900, is typified on a large scale in America. The color scheme is of the most delicate resda green and dull gold. Such painters as E. Y. Simmons and Robert Blum, sculptors, George Gray, Hugh Tallant and Enid Yandell and such designers as Wenzel and Ostertag have worked in harmony and with inspiration! The allied arts of painting, sculpture and architecture have, through their exponents, combined to produce a result that astonishes and delights, and whose effect and feeling are that of permanence, durability and extreme beauty.

Today the New Amsterdam still stands, its facade defaced by a monumental marquee, its lobby a blaze of chrome and

'At the foot of Montmartre'. An early set by Urban for the Boston Opera's 1912 production of *Louise* by Charpentier. *Columbia University Collection*

Urban's setting for Edward Seldon's play *Garden of Paradise*. It was the designs for this 1915 New York production that first brought Urban to Ziegfeld's attention. *Columbia University Collection*

34

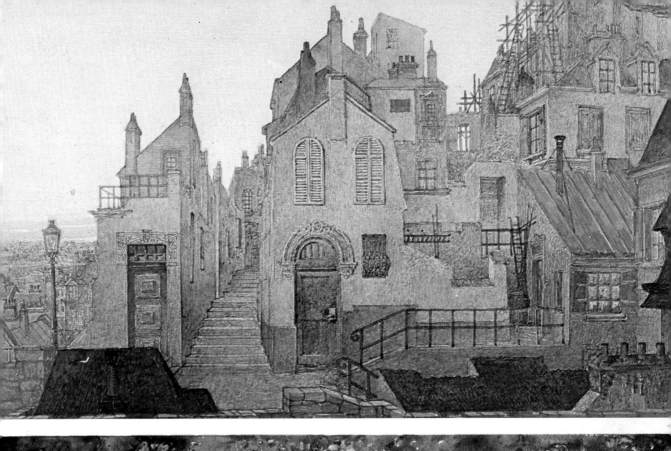

EDWARD SHELDON
THE GARDEN
OF PARADISE

E. Y. Symmon's mural over the proscenium of the New Amsterdam Theatre

Urban's exotic costumes for *Garden of Paradise. N.Y. Public Library*

mirrors. Within, however, if one looks closely, remnants of its former splendor are still discernable beneath the grime and tarnish.

The *Ziegfeld Follies* moved into the New Amsterdam in 1913. The magnificent stage and equipment lent themselves to spectacular effects, but the elements of painting, sculpture and architecture so successfully blended in the auditorium were hardly evident on stage. Ziegfeld was yet to find a designer who could invest his lavish productions with any real elegance or style. Theatre, both in England and America, had not yet, as on the Continent, attracted or for that matter, proved hospitable to artists.

In Paris, even before the turn of the century, such graphic artists as Serusier, Denis, Ibels, Egerov, Ranson, Vuillard and Toulouse-Lautrec had worked on posters or decor for plays by Maeterlinck, Hauptmann and Alfred Jarry. In Germany Max Reinhardt had employed the German impressionist painter, Louis Corinth, for his sensational productions of Wilde's *Salome* and Hofmannsthal's *Elektra*. In his 1906 production of Ibsen's *Ghosts* and the 1907 production of *Hedda Gabler*, Edward Munch's expressive lines undulated through the

37

decor, perhaps interpreting the plays even more powerfully than Reinhardt's direction.

When Diaghilev, then special assistant for the Imperial Russian Ballet, encouraged such artists as Golovine and Korovine to design for the ballet, the artist and critic Benois wrote in 1902: 'Now at last we see real painting in the theatre instead of backgrounds supplied by professional scene painters. It is an event of great importance; it foretells a total rebirth of the art of the stage in this country.' Subsequently, of course, his fusion of theatre and the plastic arts with Benois, Leon Bakst, Natalia Gontcharova, Mikhail Larionov, Picasso, Derain, Braque, Matisse, Utrillo and other artists did much to revolutionize stage design.

Joseph Urban, was barely known in New York until Flo—or, to be exact, Gene Buck—discovered him in 1914. But he was hardly a parvenu. Born in Vienna in 1872, by the age of twenty-six he had designed a castle for Count Esterhazy in Hungary, the exhibition building of the Hagenbund in Vienna, the Czar bridge over the Neva River at Petrograd, decorated the Abdin Palace for the Khedive of Egypt, illustrated several German books including Grimm's Fairy Tales, Hans Christian Andersen and Die Nibelungen. In 1898 he built and decorated three pavilions for the Kaiser's Jubilee Exposition for which he was awarded the Gold Cross, and in 1899 he won another medal for his design of the Austrian Exhibition in Venice.

Urban's connection with the stage began at the Vienna Burg Theatre, and between 1904 and 1912 he designed over fifty productions in some of the foremost theatres in Europe, including the Vienna Royal Opera, the Champs Elysées Opera in Paris and Covent Garden in London. In 1912 he was persuaded to come to America as stage director for the Boston Opera. At first the rather staid Boston critics were dismayed by his experiments in New Stagecraft as exemplified by Gordon Craig and Appia, neither of whom were as well versed in coping with the practical problems of commercial production.

Urban's aim was always to find the over-all tone, color and atmosphere by emphasizing essentials, working for effect by the simplest means and dispensing with hackneyed tricks of decoration and false perspective. His sets for *Pelléas and Mélisande* were described by a contemporary critic as 'made

The façade of the New Amsterdam Theatre, which opened in 1906. *N.Y. Public Library*

RIGHT, ABOVE: The very ornate interior of the auditorium and a detail of the mouldings

RIGHT BELOW: The Green Room

38

of strange, shadowed and sun-flecked glimpses of wood and fountain, tower, grotto and castle, vivid in varied color, full of the soft unworldliness of Debussy's music.'

During the next two years, until the war disrupted the Boston Opera in 1914, Urban introduced original elements and techniques, standard today, but not previously employed in America. The portals, first seen in his unique production of the *Tales of Hoffmann,* are described by Kenneth Macgowan in *The New Stagecraft* as

ABOVE, LEFT: Part of the auditorium, showing the boxes, in the New Amsterdam

ABOVE: Detail showing the mouldings of the staircase

40

The vandalised façade of the New Amsterdam as it is today. A movie house, the lobby is now a blaze of chrome and mirrors. *Dave Loffert*

OVERLEAF: Joseph Urban. *Courtesy Gretl Urban*

Urban's prizewinning design, submitted in an open competition in 1898, for a bridge connecting the Musik Verein building with the Vienna Concert Hall. *Columbia University Collection*

Narrow walls set at right angles to the footlights, framing the sides of the stage and connected at the top by a strip the same width. When indicated, the portals proper, at the sides, are narrowed so that the huge stage space becomes reduced to reasonable proportions. The horizontal strip at the top rids us of the worse convention of our theatre, the sky borders, or parallel strips of cloth used to represent the sky and hide the rafters.

Another of Urban's impressive innovations was his use of platforms. The rooms in *Pelléas and Mélisande* were raised two or three feet above the footlights and, as a consequence, the setting seemed smaller and more intimate; on the other hand, in the *Tales of Hoffmann,* the platform, built on a larger scale

41

and lighted in a different manner, gave the opposite effect of
distance and space.

The most striking element in Urban's work was his use of
color. He applied his paints to the canvas by the use of
pointillage, a technique employed by many artists of the
Impressionist school, but new to scenic design. Avoiding solid
colors, in the manner of Monet and Seurat, he achieved
magical effects with lighting, an art which was rudimentary at
that period and to which Urban also made an enormous
contribution. The Boston crew was not altogether happy about

Urban's design for *Riviera Girl*.
Columbia University Collection

PREVIOUS PAGE, ABOVE: Book
illustration for a special edition of
the *Niebelungen* legend done by
Urban and Lefler in 1906.
Author's Collection

BELOW: Urban's setting for *Here
Comes Tootsi*, 1915. *Columbia
University Collection*

Urban's set for the 1915 Follies. *Columbia University Collection*

his system of *pointillage*. A complex of scaffolds had to be constructed above the canvas, and the disgruntled craftsmen complained that it was like 'painting the Sistine Chapel from above.'

After reading a play or libretto meticulously, Urban would make a detailed ground plan for each scene. Next he sketched small but accurate drawings in color of his conception of the scene. From the ground plans and sketches small scale models were constructed. Many of these models are in the Urban Collection at Columbia University. When photographed they are practically indistinguishable from the actual stage settings.

When the Boston Opera closed at the beginning of World War I, Urban was offered a lucrative post designing advertizing for a shoe manufacturer, but for a smaller fee he chose to do settings and costumes for a play, *The Garden of Paradise*, by Edward Seldon. From all the reports *The Garden of Paradise* was a dismal evening in spite of Urban's dazzling settings

45

which harked back to the fairy-tale tone of his early illustrations. Gene Buck had heard rumors of the miracles performed by Urban in Boston. One look at the production and he collared Ziegfeld, who wasn't partial to other producers' shows even when unsuccessful, and dragged him into *The Garden of Paradise*. Ziegfeld knew at once that here was the artist he was searching for. He sent word to Urban that he'd like to have him 'fix his roof.' 'Does he mean,' inquired Urban with some asperity, 'that he's got a leak?'

The 'roof' turned out to be a room at the top of the New Amsterdam Theatre. *The Midnight Frolic* was Ziegfeld's latest folly, or so everyone thought, until it became a world-famous attraction, a prime training ground for potential stars and a source of ideas for the major *Follies* downstairs. Dancing, inter-table telephones, after-theatre suppers and fine liquors were featured. *The Midnight Frolic* was the forerunner of the modern floor show and it flourished until 1922 when it succumbed to the anathema of Prohibition. Urban turned the

ABOVE AND RIGHT: Set and costumes designed by Urban for *Garden of Paradise* 1914. *N.Y. Public Library*

46

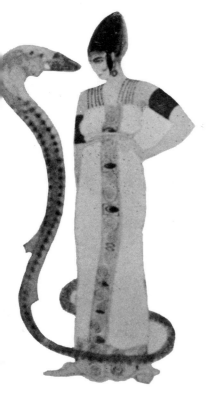

roof into a glittering night-club with a moveable stage, glass balconies and cross lighting to create stunning rainbow effects. Flo was not unaware of artistic developments abroad, and until the advent of Joseph Urban he was dissatisfied with his productions. Fanny Brice and the great negro comic, Bert Williams, had joined the festivities, but the framework of the *Follies* continued basically the same, burlesque with vaudeville specialities, and Flo was more depressed than exhilarated by his success. His private life was also onerous. The break with Anna had left a residue of bitterness, and his relationship with Lillian Lorraine, frustrating at best, had degenerated into scenes of mutual recrimination and drunken tantrums. It was at this unhappy juncture that Billie Burke put in a magical appearance.

Billie Burke (Mary William Ethelbert Appleton Burke) was born in 1885 in New Orleans, the daughter of Billie Burke, an internationally famous circus clown when circus clowns were artists, and Blanche Beatty, the daughter of a distinguished Southern family.

It is interesting to speculate on how many famous stars— Mary Pickford, Helen Hayes, Lillian and Dorothy Gish, Elsie Janis, Judy Garland, Elizabeth Taylor, June Havoc and

Gypsy Rose Lee, to name a few—might never have been heard of but for a mother's guiding, in some instances, gripping hand. Mrs. Burke was ambitious, never lost her grip, and remorselessly guided her charming but slightly apathetic daughter toward a theatrical career. So skilful were her manoeuvres, and so spontaneous Billie's talent, that by eighteen Billie Burke was a London celebrity, due to her performance in *Mrs. Ponderberry's Past* with Sir Charles Hawtrey, a leading actor-manager of the day.

In 1907 (co-incidentally the year of the first *Follies*) Charles Frohman repatriated Billie for a trifle from the French, *My Wife*, in which she supported the great matinee idol, John Drew, uncle to the three Barrymores, Ethel, John and Lionel. From the first rehearsal Drew adored her (which was not his habit) and soon she too was calling him 'uncle'. Audiences were also captivated by her red hair and roguish charm.

The next season when Billie opened in *Love Watches*, Frohman, The Starmaker, put her name up in lights. A series of frivolous comedies followed, *Mrs. Dot, The Philosopher In The Apple Orchard, The Runaway, The Mind-The-Paint-Girl, The Amazons*. Frohman produced them all in his beautiful Empire Theatre after which they toured the major cities. Billie's mother, who always accompanied her, was delighted when she entered department stores in even such remote areas as Atlanta, Georgia, to find they were selling 'Billie Burke Curls' and 'Billie Burke Dresses' (with flat lace collars). Billie had, of course, innumerable admirers, including Sir James Barrie, who once kissed her under the ear, and The Great Caruso who serenaded her in the Hotel Turaine in Boston.

The most remarkable thing about the meeting of Billie Burke and Florenz Ziegfeld is that two such celebrated figures had never met before. At 2:00 a.m. on New Year's Day, 1914, Somerset Maugham, in whose play, *The Land of Promise*, Billie was starring, escorted her to a costume ball given by the Sixty Club at the Waldorf-Astoria. They were not in costume, having enjoyed a late after-performance supper. Billie was dressed in a lovely gown designed by Lucile (Lady Duff-Gordon) with tight bodice and a full, embroidered ankle-length skirt in delicate pink which clashed becomingly with her fiery hair. 'I confess I made an entrance', wrote Billie in her delightfully

BELOW: An early photo of Billie Burke, aged 22, making her début in a London comedy, *Mrs Ponderbury's Past*. She returned to America to star opposite John Drew in 1907

ISS BILLIE BURKE

ABOVE: Billie Burke. *Romano Tozzi Collection*

BELOW: Theatre poster, *c.* 1908. *N.Y. Public Library*

candid memoirs, *With A Feather On My Nose*. 'No actress in her right mind would attempt less in descending a staircase on the arm of Somerset Maugham.'

'At the foot of the stairs stood this man. . . . He had a Mephistophelean look, his eyebrows and his eyelids lifting, curved upward, in the middle. Slim and tall and immaculate, in full evening dress, he was in black and white contrast to the rest of the costumed party; and so—and for who knows what other reasons—I noticed him at once. William Maugham and I swept on and began to dance.'

Ziegfeld had accompanied Lillian Lorraine to the ball. They quarreled and she left in a pet. Ziegfeld had been attempting to reach her by telephone, but Lillian was relegated to the past, at least temporarily, by the vision of Billie Burke descending the staircase. She didn't dance for long with Maugham. Ziegfeld bribed the orchestra to start the Paul Jones, and every time the girls moved down the line of dancers and the whistle blew, Billie found herself in Flo's arms. He danced smoothly, expertly, but Billie's attempts at polite conversation were met with numbing monosyllables. Suddenly somebody shouted, 'Hello Flo!' Billie, curiously enough, had never been to the *Ziegfeld Follies*, but there was only one Flo . . . 'I understood then why a woman who was made-up as the Empress Josephine had been staring at us. She was utterly beautiful, strange, and dark with enormous jealous eyes which followed us around the floor. She was Anna Held.'

Billie Burke knew that she was in love and also in trouble. 'I felt the impact of his threat and charm at once. But even if I had known then precisely what tortures and frustrations were in store for me during the next eighteen years because of this man, I should have kept right on falling in love.'

The siege began. With her very considerable earnings (she received $1,500 per week plus ten per cent of the gross) Billie had purchased Burkely Crest, a concrete chateau, ugly but commodious, at Hastings-on-the-Hudson within easy commuting distance of New York. It had iron gates and was surrounded by acres of park. Flo turned up frequently, sometimes unexpectedly, and paid diligent court to Mrs. Burke who was charmed. Flo installed a private line to his office so that Billie could telephone him direct. Her dressing room was inundated with flowers. He even sent a cow up to Burkely Crest.

Opposition to the match came from a strange quarter. Charles Frohman, undisputedly the world's leading producer, controlled theatres not only in London and New York but across the entire nation. He had personally produced more than five hundred plays, sometimes as many as five or six simultaneously. And he hated Ziegfeld. He said Ziegfeld had no money, no taste and couldn't produce. Frohman had a phobia about his stars marrying or being seen in public. When one of his stars, Edna May, married without his consent and hopefully sent an invitation: 'Will be at home after five,' Frohman replied, 'So will I.' In opposing the match he made it clear that if Billie married he would produce no more plays for her, his office would have nothing to do with her and she would be ruined. Billie reminded him that she had kept her promise to work for five years without getting married and that now she had a right to do as she pleased. He remained adamant and his intransigence was a decisive factor in her decision to go through with the marriage. It took place in Hoboken, New Jersey on a Saturday afternoon, between the matinée and evening performances. Frohman had left his hat in Billie's dressing room to remind her not to 'do anything foolish.' During an intermission in the performance that night she looked up and saw his funny looking little hat hanging there. She hoped she had not hurt him too much. She never saw him again.

On 1 May 1915 Frohman sailed on the *Lusitania* to pay a visit to James M. Barrie, a playwright whom he had fostered and one of his few friends. The world was shocked when the liner was torpedoed in the Irish Sea. Standing on the deck of the floundering ship Frohman remarked: 'What I don't like about this is the water will be so cold.' His brother Daniel, writing later about Charles' last moments gives a rather chilling obituary: 'It was through Rita Jolivet, now married to a wealthy Englishman, that his final words have been preserved: 'Why fear death? It is the most beautiful adventure in life.' These words were undoubtedly suggested by one of the acts in *Peter Pan* where Peter says: 'To die will be an awfully big adventure!' And Daniel concludes,

Billie Burke: a poster (*c.* 1927) used when she appeared in her husband's new theatre

50

ZIEGFELD THEATRE

Billie Burke

HAL PHYFE

I was told that his death was not caused by drowning but that, before being immersed in the water, he was killed by some heavy object that fell on him. My own impression about Charles' death is that it occurred at just about the right time. He had reached the climax of his magnificent career. Had he continued he would have had trouble, financially and otherwise. As it was he died at the top and left behind him a splendid record of theatrical achievement.

Immediately after their marriage Billie was introduced to Ziegfeld's close associate, Gene Buck, a librettist and song writer, a man of great distinction and taste, in whom Flo placed more confidence than any one else in his organization. Billie confesses to being jealous of their close friendship and to having treated him rather high-handedly. Gene Buck was to remain with Ziegfeld up to the final *Follies* in 1931, acting as ace scout and principal librettist. *The Follies* would never have achieved their fabulous success without his many innovations and his resourcefulness. Billie, of course revised her attitude. Like Anna, she was to discover more legitimate targets for jealousy. 'I was destined to be jealous of the entire *Follies* chorus as well as the *Follies* star list for the rest of my married life.'

Gene Buck's first association in the 1912 edition of the *Follies* was not entirely happy. He had created a big production number for Lillian Lorraine entitled, 'Daddy Has A Sweetheart and Mother Is Her Name', and more than five thousand dollars had been spent on costumes alone. Abe Erlanger, who was backing the show, became impatient during the tryout in Philadelphia when Lillian (whom he despised) had trouble with a costume change and was late for her entrance. He cut the number sight unseen. In 1912 even Ziegfeld didn't dare oppose Abe Erlanger. Both Gene and Lillian were sacked. They took the number over to Oscar Hammerstein's vaudeville emporium, the Victoria, where, without chorus or scenery, it was a smash hit. The song itself sold close to a million copies. That was a figure Erlanger could appreciate. The following season they were both back in the *Follies*.

Gene Buck had a sharp eye for talent. He discovered Ed Wynn in a Brooklyn vaudeville house, John Steel (the John McCormack of revue) in a church choir, Frisco dancing in a

Another Urban set for *Garden of Paradise*. *Columbia University Collection*

An Urban set from 'Behold thy Wife', 1915. *Columbia University Collection*

52

BEHOLD
THY
WIFE.
III·ACT·

Chicago basement; he roped W. C. Fields into the *Follies* against Ziegfeld's better judgment. But without doubt his greatest discovery was Joseph Urban. Against the splendor of Urban's settings in the room at the top of the New Amsterdam, *The Midnight Frolic*, several new stars emerged. Will Rogers made his debut there and Eddie Cantor was given a one night try out and remained for twenty-seven weeks. Society

A sketch of Gene Buck, Flo's right-hand man for many years. *Courtesy of ASCAP*

LEFT: 'The Garden of Eden': Urban's set for the Prologue of *The Century Girl*, a Ziegfeld/Dillingham musical of 1916. *Columbia University Collection*

portrait painter, Ben Ali Haggin's living pictures, 'posed by a bevy of Ziegfeld beauties' and featuring discreet nudity, were unveiled. And here were first seen the glamorous creations of Lucile, Lady Duff-Gordon, displayed by her frosty, detached models.

Lady Duff-Gordon's position as the supreme arbiter of women's fashion had been established in 1900, when, under

55

the sponsorship of Margot Asquith, she opened her elegant
salon, *Lucile's*, on Hanover Square in London. She introduced
the term *chic* into the language, (she later admitted that it had
often been sadly abused) and was also responsible for the
evolution of the live mannequin. Live mannequins were
employed in Paris, but they were not permitted to move and
were also encased from neck to toe in black satin. She was
horrified at Paris showings in the late Nineties to see beautiful
girls dressed in lovely gowns in pastel shades, their necks and
arms encased in dingy satin. She rounded up beautiful girls
from all over, instructed them in proper deportment, and,
gorgeously gowned in her latest creations, let them slowly
descend the steps of the beautiful Adam's room on Hanover
Square. Tea was served and the fashion show with dress
parade was born.

Lady Duff-Gordon's career in America began with a
Christmas dinner for Elsie de Wolfe (later Lady Mendl) at the
Waldorf-Astoria in 1909. The restaurant was crowded with
the most elegant women in New York, but Lucile and Elsie
noted that most of their gowns were copies of Paris models
chosen indiscriminately and without taste.

'You have no idea how much they cost,' said Elsie. 'We pay
far more here for clothes than in Europe, but we have no really
good designers.'

'Some of these women are extraordinarily attractive,'
observed Lucile, 'but they don't know how to dress. I wish I
could teach them.'

'Why don't you! I have a splendid idea. The first English
Lady of Title to open a dress shop for the Four Hundred!
Everyone will flock to you at first just for the sake of being
dressed by a woman with an English title. Afterwards, of
course, you will stand on your own merits—people will come
because they like your clothes.'

Lady Duff-Gordon wasted no time. In the Spring she
returned to New York with a collection of one hundred and
fifty gowns and four of her choice mannequins, Gamela,
Corisande, Florence and Phyllis. (Gamela and Phyllis ended
up in the *Follies*.) Gamela was described in the press as 'tall
and shapely and stately, her unfathomable eyes shining with
light.' Corisande was 'exquisitely English, fair and slim, pink

57

and white, graceful and sweet and gentle, who ought to sit dreamy-eyed on a marble seat in an old world garden thinking unutterable and tender thoughts.' Of Florence it was said that 'her eyes are wandering diamonds and her smile is born of wit. She is life. She is Spring—with a dazzle of sauciness.' And it was suggested that Phyllis 'should be placed in a picture frame at once. She should hold a young lamb and lift up her eyes to heaven forever.' Collectively the girls were described as ' "Crusaders of the Dress" given a mission of mercy, the great mission of spreading among New York's Four Hundred the cult of the dream dress, the wonderous product of the genius of Lady Duff-Gordon.'

In her memoirs Lady Duff-Gordon explains with rare delicacy and insight: 'The one thing that counts in America is self-advancement of the most blatant sort. Publicity which we would set down as incredibly bad taste is only taken as a matter of course there. . . . I could never quite get used to this, although in time I learnt to understand, learnt even to take advantage of it.' Ever perceptive, her observations on the behaviour of American women are frequently illuminating. As a passenger on the ill-fated maiden voyage of the *Titanic* (fortunately this time she was traveling without mannequins) amid scenes of indescribable horror on the decks of the sinking vessel, she yet paused to note: 'Even in that terrible moment, I was filled with wonder at nearly all of the American wives who were leaving their husbands for the lifeboats without a word of protest or regret, scarcely a farewell. They have brought the cult of chivalry to such a pitch in the States that it comes as second nature to the men to sacrifice themselves and their women to let them do it.' (And see further Appendix I for the story of the Duff-Gordons and the *Titanic* disaster.)

Fashion magazines of the period are awash with fluid pronouncements in prose worthy of her equally famous sister, the noted novelist, Eleanor Glyn. In the December 1915 issue of *Harpers Bazaar*, Lucile overflowed:

> The boudoir fantasies of a dainty woman are ever a delightful theme; I write of them with pleasure. This winter the dressing gown is a dream of coziness and beauty. I'm using for its outer surface a soft, silky material called 'zenana' which I line with a blanket-like wool of matching color. Broad bands of satin bind

the sleeves, neck, front panels and hem. Pink in its lovely range of flesh to deepest rose, I use for these *robes intimes*, as well as the paler hues.

For the belle who would seek her couch without delay, but would read awhile before she sleeps, I have designed a dear little bed jacket of warm velvet. In deep rose bordered with ermine, it is inexpressibly adorable. Even at the season's height the gayest of belles dines occasionally at home. For her domestic moods I have created trailing gowns of net sleeved and panelled with velvet and warmly collared with fur. You ask me for a prophecy: I rejoice in the newest trend of fashion —the return of frills and bows and furbelows. Nowhere are these lovelier, nowhere are they more appropriate, than a diaphanous dressing gown and dainty negligees destined for the South.

It was Billie Burke who first led Ziegfeld to Lady Duff-Gordon's Salon on 57th Street. It is probable that Flo was impressed by her latest collection (Billie ordered a couple of enchanting creations), but he was positively stunned by one stately model, Dolores, whose perfect body was breath-taking in an Eastern gown of brocade which glimmered like an opal with every movement. Lady Duff-Gordon had spotted Dolores—all of Lucile's models were identified by a single name—working as an errand girl in her London Salon. Her name was Kathleen Rose. Her posture was poor, her clothes dowdy, her speech common, but Lucile's gimlet eye detected a fabulous potential. It took a year but, Pygmalion-like, Lucile created Dolores. In a very real sense Dolores was handed to Ziegfeld ready made, for she was probably the most sensational beauty ever to appear in the *Follies*. In appreciation Ziegfeld re-created the event of her discovery in a number entitled 'Ladies of Fashion, An Episode in Chiffon.' It included nine models but it was Dolores as 'Empress of Fashion, The Discourager of Hesitancy' who took the town by storm.

Unlike many Ziegfeld show girls and stars the Dolores story has a happy ending. In May 1923, accompanied by a mountain of luggage, she sailed away on the *Olympic*. 'She'll come back,' remarked Ziegfeld, 'They always do.' But she didn't. In Paris she married multi-millionaire sportsman and art patron, Tudor Wilkinson who stated: 'There will be no honeymoon. We hope that the whole of our lives will be one long honeymoon.' They

Dolores, one of Lucile's top models, portrayed by Alfred Cheney Johnston. *Town and Country*

59

moved into a Paris apartment occupying three floors, furnished with rare antiques and drenched in Renaissance atmosphere. When interviewed in 1935, Dolores declared in cultivated British accents: 'I have made marriage and our home my career. I never enjoyed any success as much as I enjoy being an efficient housewife.'

Dolores was by no means the only contribution Lady Duff-Gordon made to Ziegfeld glamour. It was Lucile who introduced the concept of the Show Girl (simply to look beautiful and wear beautiful clothes) in contrast to the chorus girl. A number of other Lucile models went into the *Frolic* and graduated to the *Follies*, among them, Gamela, Dinagarde, Clarie, Mauricette, Anangaraga, Sovia-Moria, Boneta, Iseult, Majanah and Phyllis. Their regal manner and astonishing hauteur were helpful in maintaining proper decorum at the *Midnight Frolic* where liquor flowed rather freely; their cool majesty ultimately became the trademark of Ziegfeld's Glorified Girls. Dolores, of course, never smiled, but the others were permitted an occasional faint glimmer.

Lucile's superb designs were another important factor, though she had endless quarrels with Joseph Urban, Ziegfeld's 'aide-de-camp' as she called him. To her mind he had an 'unaccountable partiality for "yellow lights"' (amber). She wanted blue lights as a background with a white flood on each dress as it appeared, and she frequently got what she wanted.

Irene Castle, herself no mean pace-setter—it was she who discarded corsets and popularized bobbed hair—likened one of Lucile's famous gowns to a Fragonard:

It was the first dress with a torn hem line and was made of a blue-gray chiffon that looked like smoke with twelve yards around the bottom. The bodice was silver with long, full chiffon sleeves, carrying a wide band of gray fox at the wrist. The cloak was made of a blue-gray and silver brocade (using the wrong side) very full in the skirt, with a tight bodice that laced down the left side with chartreuse and emerald-green satin streamers. The huge skirt-part of this handsome brocaded cloak was garlanded in light gray fox, which had been tinted slightly mauve. Besides being beautiful, the dress was perfect for dancing. It moulded the legs and trailed out behind like smoke, giving a fluid grace to anything you did in it.

Irene Castle wears one of Lucile's most exotic gowns. Probably no dress worn on the American stage attracted more attention. *N.Y. Public Library*

60

Probably no dress ever worn on the American stage attracted more attention. The next day people were waiting in line at Lucile, Ltd. to order copies. Before the week was over ninety of them had been shipped to California, and scores, in varying colors, were sold in New York. The Metropolitan Museum even requested the gown as a part of its permanent collection.

Ziegfeld and Lady Duff-Gordon were ideally suited. Ziegfeld was willing to spend exorbitant sums on costumes, and Lady Duff-Gordon was equally extravagant. Like Ziegfeld, she was unwilling to compromise (she employed only the finest imported materials for her designs, hand-made flowers and real lace trimmings for petticoats). And, like Ziegfeld, when the Depression struck, Lucile, Ltd. folded. A manufacturer of Levantine persuasion took over the business, the salon on Hanover Square was also abandoned, and Lady Duff-Gordon retired to Hampstead Heath to compose her memoirs, *Discretions and Indiscretions*.

A Study of a
GREENWICH VILLAGE FOLLIES
ARTIST MODEL *by*
W.T. Benda
The Eminent American Artist

3
Follies—
and
More Follies

Olive Thomas, 'a rare beauty with a delicate, heart-shaped face', whose liason with Flo caused much press comment before she finally married Mary Pickford's brother.
N.Y. Public Library

THE CAST FOR THE 1915 FOLLIES INCLUDED W. C. FIELDS, Ed Wynn, Ina Claire, Ann Pennington, Bert Williams, Leon Errol, Mae Murray, George White, Olive Thomas, Kay Laurell and Justine Johnstone, but the real star was Joseph Urban. Like the artists designing for Diaghilev's *Ballets Russes,* Urban did more than merely create a frame for the performers. To be sure, he provided the continental elegance Ziegfeld had been searching for, his architectural stage decor was new, the opulence astonishing, the entire physical production polished to a lustre, but in a very real sense the crude, even naive patterns of the early *Follies* began to reflect Urban's sophistication and artistry. Ziegfeld was well aware of Urban's enormous contribution, and during the rest of his career had an almost superstitious fear of attempting any production without Urban's collaboration.

For the *Ziegfeld Follies of 1915* Urban created a shimmering underwater sequence for Kay Laurell as The Channel Belle. He satisfied Ziegfeld's mania for elephants in the 'Gates of Elysium' with towering elephants flanking the center entrance and spouting water. His 'America' was a riot of reds, whites and blues with Olive Thomas as the 'Dove of Peace.' For a flag-waving finish, (patriotism was rife that season) Justine Johnstone posed as Columbia. The Ziegfeld Parade presented 'A Girl For Every Month of The Year' and W. C. Fields, who was given lines for the first time, socked Ed Wynn over the head with a billiard cue claiming he was stealing laughs. The box office was besieged, the stage door mobbed and the *Midnight Frolic* a riot.

And it was also in 1915 that the ever alert Gene Buck discovered an ascetic young art student, Alfred Cheney Johnston, who was also an amateur photographer. Flo suggested that he abandon his art studies and turn to photography as a serious profession. As official photographer of the *Follies*, a post he maintained throughout Ziegfeld's career, Johnston's stylish photographs truly immortalized the Ziegfeld Girl.

While all this splendour was being created, Billie Burke was in Hollywood making a picture called *Peggy* for Thomas H. Ince. She played the part of a Scottish lass who dressed as a boy. There were all sorts of delays while a fishing village and chapel were being constructed where the road winds down from Topanga Canyon to the Pacific. During this interval, disturbing rumors reached her about Flo's involvement with Olive Thomas, a rare beauty with a delicate, heart-shaped face and deep blue eyes. There was comment in the newspapers and friends contributed interesting anecdotes concerning yachting parties, even going so far as to wire asking point blank when she intended to divorce Flo. Billie was particularly incensed, having just turned down a five-year contract with Ince, realizing that she couldn't hope to stay in Hollywood and remain Mrs. Florenz Ziegfeld Jr. She fled to San Francisco where Flo joined her, and they quarreled for two days; that is to say Billie quarreled while Flo sat quietly puffing cigars, imperturbable even when she tore down draperies and threw china. 'The trouble with you Billie,' he finally announced, 'is

ABOVE: W. C. Fields, who starred in the 1915 *Follies*, photographed in 1925. *N.Y. Public Library*

ABOVE, RIGHT: A retouched publicity shot of W. C. Fields for the 1925 *Follies*. *N.Y. Public Library*

BELOW, RIGHT: Another member of the 1915 *Follies* cast, Mae Murray, seen here in the film *Peacock Alley*, made in 1922. *N.Y. Museum of Modern Art*

PAGES 66/7
TOP LEFT: Urban's set for a bath scene in the 1915 *Follies*, featuring one of Flo's enduring passions — elephants. *Columbia University Collection*

BELOW, LEFT, AND RIGHT: Three of Urban's sets for the 1916 *Follies*. *Columbia University Collection*

that when you accuse me, you always pick the wrong girl.' Whether or not Olive was the wrong girl, the matter was resolved when Olive departed for Hollywood, achieved considerable success in films and married Jack Pickford, brother of America's Sweetheart, Mary. The marriage proved stormy. Finally, alone in Paris, Jack having fled to London, Olive died after swallowing several tablets of bichloride of mercury, whether by accident or intent has never been determined.

Billie made another film, *Gloria's Romance*. This one, a serial, was shot in Florida. On her return the newspapers reported discreetly, that 'Billie Burke, in private life Mrs. Florenz Ziegfeld Jr., has retired temporarily from her busy stage and screen life to await an interesting event.' Patricia Ziegfeld was born 23 October 1916 in Ziegfeld's thoroughly sanitized suite —Billie distrusted hospital hygiene—in the Hotel Ansonia.

The child had blue eyes and curly red hair and was to prove

Urban's set for Edward Seldon's play *Garden of Paradise*, 1914. *N.Y. Public Library*

one of the few stabilizing influences in Ziegfeld's erratic life. Irving Berlin was Billie's first caller after Patricia's arrival. Flo, who was busy rehearsing his latest show, *The Century Girl*, wandered in later looking rather sad.

'What do you know,' he said, 'Lorraine got married. Imagine that!' Billie was not amused.

The 1916 *Follies* had opened to even greater *réclame* than the previous edition. Urban's decor included a fanciful Venetian episode, and for a travesty of Antony and Cleopatra, he projected a fabulous gray sphinx against one of his famous midnight-blue skies. (Urban had introduced the bowed cyclorama for greater depth.) In the closing scene pink roses streamed from massive vases. Lady Duff-Gordon's chiffons ran riot in 'My Lady of The Nile.' The impact of the Russian Ballet was clear. Fanny Brice sang 'Nijinsky' and Carl Randall danced 'Spectre de la Rose' with the stage filled with Ziegfeld Girls as roses. Jerome Kern had his first *Follies* song hit with 'Have A Heart' and Irving Berlin was represented with 'In

Study of a Ziegfeld beauty, Drucilla Strain, by *Follies* photographer Alfred Cheney Johnston

68

Florida Among the Palms.' Will Rogers made his first appearance in the 1916 edition and others in the superb cast included Ina Claire, Bert Williams, Lilyan Tashman, Justine Johnstone and Marion Davies who cavorted in 'I Left Her On the Beach In Honolulu.'

Immediately after the opening of the *Follies of 1916* Ziegfeld, in association with Charles Dillingham, put *The Century Girl*, a super-extravaganza, into rehearsal. It opened at the new Century Theatre on Columbus Circle on 6 November to rave reviews. Hazel Dawn, already acclaimed as the star of *The Pink Lady*, was 'The Century Girl.' Victor Herbert collaborated on the score and Urban's settings ranged from a celestial staircase on pink and lavender clouds to Grand Central Station on 42nd Street. 'A Procession of Laces of the World' served as the Grand Finale, ending in a matrimonial ceremony with all the stars joining hearts and hands. The show ran for two hundred performances.

Having taken over Broadway and been indisputably hailed as The Great Ziegfeld, Flo turned his attention to Burkely Crest. In this he was abetted by Mrs. Burke who had already expanded the grounds by the purchase of a number of acres and had erected several Japanese tea houses. He planted twenty-four towering blue spruces on either side of the driveway leading to the house, seeded meadows, laid out tennis courts and commissioned Joseph Urban to design a swimming pool which proved large enough for canoeing and contained a statue of a cherub holding a fish from which water spouted. A replica of Mount Vernon, surrounded by geranium plants, was constructed as a play house for Patricia, complete with child-sized furniture, a storey-and-a-half living room, library, bedroom and porch. There was a covered passageway to the kitchen, china cupboards and practical stove. A herd of deer was introduced, ten in all, two bears, three lion cubs, along with partridges and pheasants, all of whom had special preserves. Innumerable cockatoos and parrots occupied an aviary. Two buffaloes, one of whom immediately gave birth, moved in with a baby elephant weighing 250 pounds. There were also numerous cats, geese, lambs, three monkeys, ducks,

1917 *Follies* poster, an example of the work of Kirchner, a fine draughtsman of the period. *Romano Tozzi Collection*

RIGHT ABOVE: Urban's set for 'A Young Man's Fancy', 1919. *Columbia University Collection*

RIGHT BELOW: 'Zeppelin over London', one of Urban's sets for the 1915 *Ziegfeld Follies. Columbia University Collection*

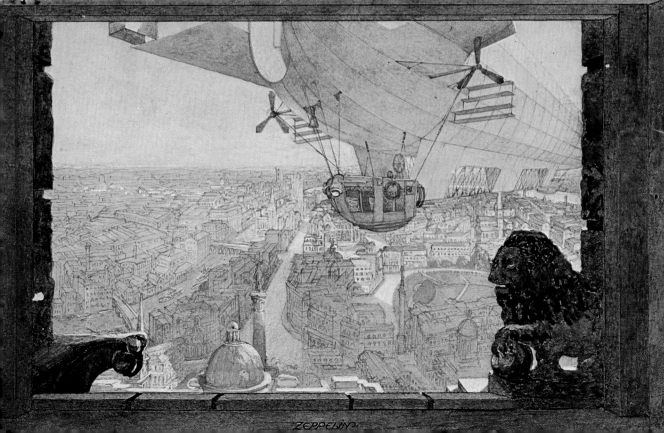

ZEPPELIN

THE·EMPEROR·OF·CRABS·

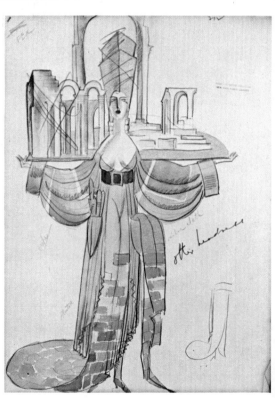

rban's design for 'Rose of China', number from the *Ziegfeld Follies*. was an unusual set, for which e used gauze curtains and ouble-deck' levels. *Columbia niversity Collection*, 1919

LOW, LEFT: 'The Emperor of abs', one of Urban's costumes for arden of Paradise. *N.Y. Public brary*

LOW, RIGHT: 'Miss Labor Day', mes Reynolds' costume from the 020 *Greenwich Village Follies*. *ew York Public Library*

PAGE 74: An Alfred Cheney Johnston portrait of Katherine Burke—he called it 'Ziegfeld Voodoo'. *N.Y. Public Library*

PAGE 75 ABOVE: Burkeley Crest, the Ziegfeld's country estate. Surrounded by lawns and trees, the vine-covered house overlooked a broad sweep of the Hudson River. *Romano Tozzi Collection*

BELOW: Billie Burke, Flo and their daughter Patricia by the side of their swimming pool, c. 1924. *Alfred Cheney Johnston*

three hundred chickens and fifteen dogs. Though flowers grew everywhere, inside the greenhouse and out, Flo had dozens of long-stemmed roses delivered daily from the local florist.

The main house—there was another for Mrs. Burke and several cottages—was manned by a staff of fifteen, augmented, of course, for entertainments, especially dinner parties which sometimes numbered as many as sixty. The latest motion pictures were frequently screened, and Flo insisted that every servant have a comfortable seat and see the entire show. On opening nights at the New Amsterdam, he reserved the front row in the mezzanine for the staff and sent them in style in special cars.

Flo was also capable of little spur-of-the-moment surprises such as having the whole house redecorated at one fell swoop by Sloane Farley, New York's most fashionable decorator. On another occasion, Billie returned to find the enormous dining room inundated with the state banquet service of the late Emperor Nicholas II, including tall vases and other decorative pieces so large that two men were required to lift them. Billie, who described herself as 'essentially the tea-cozy type,' was slightly horrified.

The relationship between the Ziegfelds and the villagers of Hastings-on-Hudson, though tinged with awe, was cordial in the extreme. Alan Brock, who grew up to be an actor and an actor's agent, recalls: 'When Miss Burke's Rolls-Royce stopped on Main Street, news spread in seconds that Miss Burke was at Neeley's. When she came out of the stationery store, a buzz of whispers filled the air, about her clothes, her red hair, her freckles or her parasol. Laughing and chatting with everyone, she would summon her chauffeur and slip him a bill, and all the kids followed him, like the Pied Piper, into Adam's Ice Cream Parlor.' One summer word got around that Billie Burke was going to take a group of village kids on a picnic to the Bronx Park, as many as her five Rolls-Royces (each of different color) could hold. 'When that wonderful morning arrived we all waited in front of the ice cream parlor. At 10:00 a.m. Miss Burke was there in the first car with her mother, also four servants to keep us in tow. The picnic was limited to kids between five and twelve. I was lucky. I was seven.'

After Ziegfeld's death, the entire estate was sold for thirty-

six thousand dollars. The house itself was torn down, but the gates and two facing columns still stand. The stone wall, more than five feet high, is beginning to crumble. Frank Bankowitz, who used to work as a teenager in the local grocery store, recalls: 'A group of us climbed a cherry tree and got caught up there by one of Ziegfeld's huge dogs. We were up there for a long time before Mr. Craig, the caretaker, called the dogs off. We used to pick violets there and sell them. What a zoo they had! All gone now. Even the gardens are grown over and the swimming pool filled in with fallen trees and trash. . . .'

On 20 January 1971 Patricia Ziegfeld Stephenson wrote to Alan Brock from Hollywood:

Thank you for sending me your article about Hastings in the Twenties. It all seems so long ago and yet so very close in my memory. I remember picking out the Christmas wreaths for our front door with real English holly full of red berries. I always hoped and prayed for snow on Christmas Eve. I remember, too, old Doc Tod in the village, his drugstore and all those amazing toys in his window. And the scent of the lilacs that grew all over the place is still with me. The things one stores away from childhood! The tiny pollywogs as they darted about in the lower brook by the stone wall. I used to sit there and watch them by the hour. . . . Thank you for jostling all those lovely memories. . . . Did you know that mother is buried at Mount Kisco at Walhalla? It was her wish. There is no plaque yet, as they have to wait for the ground to thaw. . . . I hope you'll keep me posted on all the goings on in Hastings. I'm always interested, even a bit envious. . . . .

Warmest regards,
Patricia

Flush with the success of *The Century Girl*, Ziegfeld and Dillingham laid out elaborate plans to take over the Century Theatre. The Century was a superb building in neo-roman-esque style, but because of its size and location, a problem house. Paris Singer had engaged it briefly for Isadora Duncan as a home for her school. Isadora was so appalled by the rich decor that she had the interior draped in burlap. Then she

moved in all her girls with their own beds and cooking stoves. Fire marshalls promptly moved them out. Isadora, incidentally, despised Ziegfeld and all he stood for. When one of her girls, Irma, was lured toward the *Follies*, Isadora accused Ziegfeld of 'exploiting her' and condemned her 'cheap Broadway spirit.' (Irma remained with Isadora who at that time was living in a small cottage at Long Beach frequented by artists and other distinguished people for whom she gave impromptu performances, climaxed by her incomparable parody of The Ziegfeld Girl.) After the failure of the Ziegfeld-Dillingham, *Miss 1917*, nothing much happened at The Century except for visiting ballet and opera. The magnificent structure was demolished in the late Fifties.

It is interesting to speculate on what direction the Ziegfeld-Dillingham association would have taken had the Century Theatre Project flourished. Their plans were certainly elaborate, including a restaurant night-club, scenic studio and a special costume department for Lady Duff-Gordon and Mme. Pascaud of Paris.

Miss 1917 was one of the most notable flops in Broadway history. Ziegfeld and Dillingham had known one another as young men about town in Chicago; money to Dillingham, like Ziegfeld, was confetti. In 1914 Dillingham had scored a smashing success with *Watch Your Step* which had Irving Berlin's first musical score in ragtime, the new craze, and Irene and Vernon Castle as its stars. *Stop, Look and Listen*, a second Berlin show with Gaby Deslys and Blossom Seely, had packed the mammoth Hippodrome for 426 performances. In *Miss 1917* Ziegfeld and Dillingham shot the works. Costumes by Raphael Kirchner, Pascaud and Max Weldy of Paris and Lady Duff-Gordon, fantastic settings by Joseph Urban, songs by Jerome Kern and Victor Herbert, a cast which included some of the most prominent names of the day, Lew Fields, Savoy & Brennen, Bessy McCoy, Elizabeth Brice and Charles King, Ann Pennington, Dolores, Harry Kelly, Cecil Lean, Cleo Mayfield, Flora Revalles of the Russian Ballet ('The Spirit of The Woods'), the budding prima donna, Vivienne Segal, and the rising dancer, George White. Marion Davies graduated from the chorus and spoke a few lines. Ziegfeld didn't want Irene Castle, whom he had never admired, and Irene Castle didn't want to be in it either, because she was making a movie in New Jersey and was also nervous about a solo appearance, Vernon having been recently killed in a plane crash. Dillingham insisted, and Irene agreed when offered one thousand dollars a week, with the promise that she could wear anything she liked, pick her own music, approve the sets, skip matinées and avoid the finale. In *Castles in the Air*, Irene wrote:

> I told Charley (Dillingham) I wanted to make my entrance down a long flight of stairs. When I saw my set, I gasped. It was one of Joseph Urban's most perfect creations. Flanking the silver stairs were two huge mauve chiffon pillars, lighted from within, and the staircase curved up to a Maxfield Parrish blue sky. Little did I know I would be descending directly from heaven into hell.

The elaborate, talent-heavy production wouldn't fit together at dress rehearsal. Dillingham and Ziegfeld spent the night reshuffling the numbers, chopping sequences, tearing their hair, yelling at the artists and at each other. Opening night was even more dreadful. Everything went wrong. One of the mauve columns got stuck, and Irene's entrance was delayed twenty minutes. The singer currently performing was signaled to stretch his act while Ziegfeld, backstage, raved and ranted like Simon Legree among his slaves. The final curtain descended at 1:30 a.m.

Miss 1917 floundered through a couple of weeks and finally sank on a rainy Wednesday night leaving a wake of law suits. Irene lost her staircase after the first performance and later was even locked out of her dressing room. The courts finally awarded her her full salary two years later.

Though *Miss 1917* was the show Ziegfeld most wanted to forget, it caused him to take an ever tighter grip on future productions. The staging of the early *Follies* had been largely the work of the brilliant Julian Mitchell with Ziegfeld more in the roll of promoter, but Ned Wayburn, who had joined the organization in 1915, was equally talented and possibly an even better organizer. Rehearsal discipline became increasingly rigid, and Ziegfeld's mania for perfection of detail, pacing and balance fused the myriad elements of the revue into a perfect unit. The truly great *Follies*, beginning with the 1918 edition and culminating in the 1922 edition, achieved

LEFT AND RIGHT: Song sheets of popular *Follies* hits of the early Twenties

PREVIOUS PAGES: Four panels drawn by Kirchner and posed by Ziegfeld Girls for a series of pictures entitled 'The Seven Deadly Sins'

78

perfection through the highest skill of production; for opulence and splendor, nothing to quite equal them has been seen before or since.

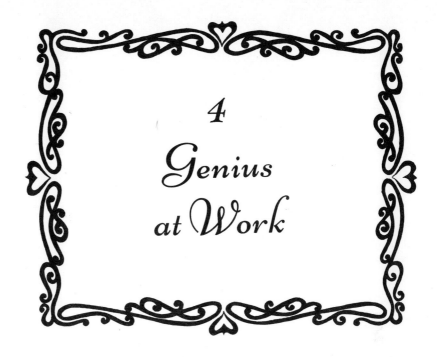

4
Genius at Work

ATTEMPTING TO GRASP THE GENIUS OF ZIEGFELD IS SOMEWHAT like probing a mist. He had little feeling for music, and though he employed some of the leading comics of the day, he had slight appreciation of their art. While chiefly celebrated for his love of female beauty and a passion for exploiting it, this was only one element. In the final analysis he was, perhaps, something of a Midas who converted gross into gold to fashion a fitting crown for his own superb ego. It would be hard to say whether this alchemy was achieved at greater cost to himself, his associates or his backers. In any event, Ziegfeld was not an easy man to work for or with.

In his book *Showman*, William A. Brady, the noted producer, whose association with Ziegfeld was obviously purely social, observed: 'It was a treat to watch Ziegfeld studying out a new production with samples of materials spread out in front of him and costume designs, light plots, scripts and actors'

An Alfred Cheney Johnston study: Merle Finley of the *Follies*

pictures all over the room—raw material that would be whittled into an integrated whole by the time rehearsals started.'

As a matter of fact, very little was actually whittled down or integrated by the time rehearsals started. All of Ziegfeld's *Follies* were built rather than conceived. His writers were driven mad. Channing Pollock and Rennold Wolf, when working on the 1915 *Follies*, were sent fifty pounds of loose paper with jotted notes and suggestions in Ziegfeld's sprawling hand. While they were attempting to decipher them, they were bombarded by telephone calls at all hours of the day and night and badgered with telegrams, sometimes thousands of words in length. Arriving with twenty or more skits, they discovered that Joseph Urban had created stage sets ordered by Ziegfeld, which bore no relation to the material agreed upon. New material had to be fashioned to fit Urban's designs. The diving star Annette Kellerman was replaced by Ina Claire. The twenty-five-thousand-dollar Roman pool designed for Annette was converted into a background for undraped beauties, but new sketches had to be invented for Ina, also for W. C. Fields and Ed Wynn who were suddenly hired. 'We wrote a library,' Pollack observed, 'and produced a pamphlet.' P. G. Wodehouse and Guy Bolton found themselves in a similar predicament, except in their case they wrote material to fit designs only to find that the designs had been discarded. Ring Lardner's experiences with Ziegfeld were also calamitous, but Lardner retaliated by writing *A Day With Conrad Green*, an acid little tale depicting the producer as a petty tyrant, hypocrite and liar. Fortunately for Ziegfeld, it is not one of Lardner's more memorable efforts.

Composers fared little better; Gershwin and Romberg were expected to deliver an entire score in three weeks to the day. They did. Ziegfeld passed up Noel Coward songs as too British and too sophisticated. Kern and Friml suffered endless vicissitudes, and Victor Herbert became so furious with Ziegfeld that he succumbed to a fatal heart attack. The team of Gene Buck and Dave Stamper had the most stamina, and Irving Berlin, who could pour out melodies almost as fast as Ziegfeld demanded, had the best track record. He wrote 'A Pretty Girl Is Like A Melody' overnight as a filler for the 1919

Brinkley, a famous Twenties illustrator, produced his own version of 'The Glorification of the Ziegfeld Girl'. *Romano Tozzi Collection*

PAGES 84/85
LEFT: Will Rogers, Flo's favourite comedian and close friend. *N.Y. Public Library*

CENTER: Various Ziegfeld beauties

RIGHT: W. C. Fields—a comedian Ziegfeld abominated. *N.Y. Public Library*

THE
Glorification of the
ZIEGFELD GIRL

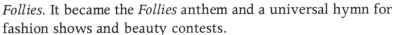

Follies. It became the *Follies* anthem and a universal hymn for fashion shows and beauty contests.

Comedians also had trouble. 'You know,' said Ziegfeld, 'I don't have a very quick sense of humor. Half the great comedians I've had in my shows and that I paid a lot of money to and who made my customers shriek were not only not funny to me, but I couldn't understand why they were funny to anybody. You'd be surprised how many of my expensive comics I've run out on and locked myself in my office when they were on stage.' Gene Buck was the great stabilizer in this department, but even he couldn't keep Ziegfeld from con-

stricting W. C. Fields, a comedian Flo abominated, especially when Fields used chorus girls as props. Ziegfeld once summoned an assistant and said, 'How long does it take the girls to dress here?' 'Seven minutes,' he was told. 'Hold your sketch to seven minutes,' he ordered Fields. At the outset Ziegfeld detested Will Rogers and told Gene Buck to fire him. The act which offended is best described by a quote on Rogers' debut from the *New York American* of 6 January 1916:

Against a sky of Egyptian blue and glimpsed marble pillars bathed in moonlight, came a gorgeous creature in a Paris ball gown who sauntered nonchalantly down the marble steps and

across the stage. Then all of a sudden a young man in shirt sleeves and chaps materialized right in the scandalized spotlight. The young man had a rope in his hand, and the rope suddenly became alive, describing fantastic circles in the air about him. The rope incircled the gorgeous creature and the oddly assorted pair began to waltz. The rope danced with them, hemmed them in, slipped under their feet skilfully and came up on the other side still whirling. Nothing that they could do embarrassed that rope. They played hop, skip and jump with it, but it always evaded them. As the lights dimmed the spinning rope glowed in phosphorescent coils.

Instead of firing him, Gene Buck suggested Rogers re-inforce his act with a 'rope of words.' At first, Rogers' barbed comments on current events and audience celebrities both frightened and horrified Ziegfeld, but audiences loved them. 'Your big butter-and-egg man,' explained Rogers, 'your authors, baseball players, and especially your politicians, like attention. They eat it up. And the folks who pay the tariff at the box-office like to know they are in prominent company. They go home and brag about sitting next to so-and-so even if they were ten rows away.'

Rogers' current comments were up to the minute, which is why most of them, if quoted, have little pertinence today. As he explained,

> At the matinée I pull stuff based on the noon editions of the afternoon papers. Well, before the evening performance all the matinée stuff is too stale for the audience, so I use the sporting editions and finals. But by the time the *Midnight Frolic* starts, these late evening jokes are also stale, so I get the first edition of the *Morning Telegraph* and make my monologue out of that. No joke can get over after it is six hours old. A lot of clever writers have tried to fix me up with acts, but I can't get away with them. I've got to make it up as I go along.

Ziegfeld eventually went along with Rogers, who became his favourite comedian and finally one of his few loyal friends.

Ziegfeld was only really in his element when his Glorified Girls populated the stage, but even these extravagant scenes were ruthlessly paced and edited. He never allowed opulence to satiate. If, for example, one or all of the *Follies* girls appeared with bosoms artistically bare, it was only for a fleeting second. As George Jean Nathan, one of Ziegfeld's most astute critics,

observed: 'Where other producers present, Ziegfeld suggests. And in this suggestion, this skimming-over-the-water quality, this technique of implication, there is much greater effectiveness than in the italics of emphasis. He steers the shrewd course of bringing sophistication and innocence into sudden, violent and hence effective collision.' And in a different context Nathan wrote:

> Take away all his tunes, all his lyrics and all his jokes and give him merely Joseph Urban, fifty or sixty girls and a keg of talcum powder and his *Follies* would be just as good a show as it is—in fact, perhaps a lot better. For Ziegfeld can dramatize girls the way no other producer can. He can take a various assortment of them, most of whom naturally or in other hands wouldn't be worth a second glance, and with that peculiar cunning of his convert them into what appear to be lovely and glamorous creatures. With silks and paint and powder and lighting, he can create the illusion of feminine beauty even where beauty isn't. It is a trick that no other producer I know of has succeeded in mastering, the proof whereof is that when these selfsame girls are seen on other revue stages they look no more like their Ziegfelded selves than their mothers do.

A body of material has been published delineating Ziegfeld's criteria for feminine beauty—shape of ankles, color of hair, measurements, etc.—some of it by Ziegfeld himself, some by his press agents and other bemused commentators, but it is entirely possible that Nathan's analysis is nearer the mark.

When producing a show Flo worked furiously in eighteen-hour shifts. He could sleep anywhere, but was seldom caught napping. 'At Burkely Crest,' Billie recounts, 'we revolved like little moons around Flo's sun, avoiding the heat when we could.' When not in his untidy offices in the New Amsterdam or at rehearsals, he worked at all hours from the eminence of his massive bed, dictating to his saintly secretary, Goldie, badgering press agents, dispatching frenetic telegrams and making thousands of notes, jabbing his pencils fiercely and hurling them across the room. The cool, public image he habitually presented vanished completely. No one but Ziegfeld had any conception of what the show would be like, but at final rehearsals he rose to full majesty, shaping, slashing and honing his *Follies* into a flawless opening night. These

LEFT ABOVE: Typical of Urban's evocative powers – a delicate example of rural nostalgia designed for the 1920 *Follies*

BELOW: In the 1921 *Follies* Urban designed a Parisian setting for Fanny Brice's famous number, 'My Man'. *Columbia University Collection*

91

exertions invariably resulted in a prolonged bilious attack.

The question has often been posed by critics, editors and other searchers after truth: What was the secret of Flo Ziegfeld? No one has yet come up with a satisfactory answer, but a decisive factor, one which can not be over emphasized, was his incredible dynamic energy. In every epoch individuals appear who are blessed or cursed with almost superhuman impulsion, Wagner, Balzac, Florence Nightingale, Adolf Hitler, to mention a few. Though their goals are disparate, they seem irresistibly propelled toward achievement or disaster or, as in the case of Ziegfeld, a combination of both. During the last bitter years, after the Wall Street crash of 1929, Flo was actually driven to the very brink of insanity; like an exploding star he literally burned himself out, his disaster no less dynamic than his success.

Billie Burke had been doing a lot of motion picture work at Famous Players Lasky Studios on Fifty-Seventh street and in Astoria, but the theatre was still her first love. In the fall of 1919, Ziegfeld found time to present her in *Caesar's Wife*, a new play by Somerset Maugham. It was an intimate little triangle concerning the wife of the British Consul in Cairo who falls in love with her husband's young secretary within a romantic Urban setting of dusky palms and sapphire sky. Dorothy Parker, who had recently joined the staff of *Vanity Fair*, didn't care for the show and concluded her rather acid notice with the observation that: 'Miss Burke is at her best in her more serious moments; in her desire to convey the girlishness of the character, she plays her lighter scenes as if she were giving an impersonation of Eva Tanguay.'

Ziegfeld, whose power was far-reaching, was incensed and complained to the publisher, Condé Nast, who called in editor, Frank Crowninshield, and told him to fire Dorothy Parker. The injustice of this outraged the budding playwright, Robert Sherwood, and also Robert Benchley, then a managing editor. Other members of the Algonquin Round Table Set, including Harold Ross, Alexander Woollcott and Tallulah Bankhead, were equally inflamed. Benchley and Sherwood both threatened to resign if Dorothy were fired, which was just what Crowninshield was hoping for. The troublesome

RIGHT: The elfin Marilyn in action. John Mason Brown called her 'Broadway's Pavlova'. *N.Y. Public Library*

BELOW: Eva Tanguay, Broadway star. Dorothy Parker accused Billie Burke of impersonating Eva's 'gushing girlishness'. *N.Y. Public Library*

trio had been out of step with *Vanity Fair* for some time. Sherwood had satirized advertisers in his column, 'What The Well Dressed Man Will Wear'; Dorothy Parker, when asked not to reveal her salary, had hung a sign around her neck stating the exact sum, and when Benchley was asked to account for being late, he filled in a tardy slip in minuscule handwriting explaining at length that he had assisted in rounding up elephants which had escaped from the Hippodrome and were threatening to board the Staten Island Ferry. The Trio placed a collection box in the lobby accompanied by a sign reading: 'Contributions for Miss Billie Burke' and walked out of *Vanity Fair*, but fortunately not into limbo.

Marilyn Miller photographed by Alfred Cheney Johnston. At the time she was starring in MGM's version of Ziegfeld's musical *Sally*. *N.Y. Public Library*

94

If imitation is the highest form of flattery, it is the only compliment the Shuberts ever paid Ziegfeld. In 1909, when J. J. Shubert got wind that Flo was about to attend a performance of their production, *The Mimic World*, J.J. informed Flo that he would be barred from the theatre. When questioned by reporters, Flo responded:

The Mimic World—that's a good title for their show. They had a lot of my stuff in it in Atlantic City and Philadelphia, 'The Soul Kiss' and 'The Genie From Baghdad.' I made them take them out. They have half my title stuck up on their marquee. *Hits of 1909*, they call it. Strangers in New York who know of the great success of the *Follies* will get mixed-up and drift in

A stylish song sheet of the Twenties. *Heide-Gillman Collection*

95

there when they want to come here. I'm not particularly anxious to see the Shubert show, but I think it's pretty cheeky all the way round.

Spurred by the success of the *Follies*, the Shuberts opened their *Passing Shows* in 1912 in the new Winter Garden under the personal direction of J. J. Shubert. *The Passing Shows* were never in Ziegfeld's class, but there was a long runway circling from the stage to the rear of the stalls and a plentiful line-up of girls with the accent on nudity. The sketches were broad and the songs snappy. The competition spurred Ziegfeld to ever greater activity. He was also not averse to luring performers away with higher salaries and *Follies* prestige. Among those who moved over to the New Amsterdam were the ravishing Jesse Reed, Nita Naldi, vamp supreme, the exquisite dancer, Mary Eaton, and Marilyn Miller. (Lucille La Sueur, who appeared as a beaded bag in a living curtain, passed up both J.J. and Ziegfeld to become MGM's Joan Crawford.) In his theatrical reminiscences, *Dramatis Personae*, the noted critic, John Mason Brown, tellingly evokes an image of Marilyn Miller. 'For me Miss Miller has never stopped dancing. She haunts me as a vision of spangles and sunshine, beautiful of body, empty of face, and supreme in grace, eternally pirouetting as Broadway's Pavlova.'

Marilyn Miller (née Mary Ellen Reynolds) was originally from Louisville, Kentucky. She had traveled all over the world with her family's vaudeville act, *The Five Columbians*, in which she was billed as Miss Sugarplum. Marilyn's voice was slight, but as Billie Burke described her, she was a 'confection of a girl, an elfin creature who presents a most enchanting effect. A delightful thing happens when she comes on stage.' Delightful things happened when Marilyn stepped on the stage at the Winter Garden, and when Ziegfeld whisked her into the 1918 *Follies* in 'Sweet Sixteen' amidst Urban's bouquets and urns, it was evident that he had discovered a major property. The Shuberts, of course, were livid. They had a five-year contract, but since Marilyn was a minor at the time of signing—it had been attested by her mother—they were unable to hold her to it.

Off-stage Marilyn was rather less delightful, nor was she easily bought. Shrewd, wilful and ambitious, she was capable

Two song sheets featuring Marilyn. Note P. G. Wodehouse's name on the lower one, as lyric writer for Ziegfeld's musical *Rosalie*. *Heide-Gillman Collection*

Girls from the *Follies*, 1922

of random cruelty, both artless and contrived. Flo was fascinated. She was willing to work hours on end to perfect her performance, but his most lavish gifts and attentions ended in total rejection. To make matters worse, he realized that she was falling in love with Frank Carter, a handsome young comedian and dancer with the build of a boxer whose number in the show was Irving Berlin's 'I'm Goin' To Pin A Medal On The Girl I Left Behind.' Marilyn and Frank were married in May of 1919.

Ziegfeld dropped Frank Carter from the *Follies* before opening, and Marilyn threw a diamond bracelet Flo had given her back in his face. Their quarrels were frequent and bitter. Word of Frank Carter's death came to Marilyn in her dressing-room by telephone. He had been killed instantly outside Cumberland, Maryland, when their new Packard, which he had just had monogramed MM & FC, crashed. Marilyn gave orders that no one was to speak to her. When her cue came she floated on stage, glittering and flawless, to deliver 'Sweet Sixteen.' Ziegfeld excused her from the show and sent her on an extended European tour.

The musical Flo planned for Marilyn during her absence was his first book show, a Cinderella story, *Sally*, tailored to her talents by Guy Bolton and P. G. Wodehouse, with a score by Jerome Kern and a Butterfly Ballet by Victor Herbert. It limned the adventures of a scullery maid, who, posing as a Russian ballerina, invades a Long Island garden party where she falls in love with a millionaire. She finally wins him, but not before she has become a star in the *Follies*. Marilyn cast a spell when she sang 'Look For The Silver Lining,' and to little Patricia Ziegfeld, who had been taken to the theatre for the first time, when Marilyn danced 'she seemed to be floating above the stage like a thistle-down angel.'

In her memoirs, *The Ziegfeld's Girl*, Patricia also describes the scene which took place backstage after performance.

'Hello you lousy son-of-a-bitch,' was Marilyn's greeting to them.

'Now dear,' replied Flo, 'I brought my little daughter backstage especially to meet you. You've heard me talk about Patricia, haven't you?'

'Yea, to the point of nausea.' He asked what was bothering

her. 'You know goddam well what's bothering me. It's this piece of crap you call a costume. It weighs a ton, and as far as I'm concerned you can take it and shove it!' Flo hastily explained that this was Patty's first show, her very first. 'How thrilling,' hissed Marilyn. 'And what the hell are you being so goddamned quaint about? You sound like Daddy Longlegs.'

Flo hustled Patricia out. As the door closed behind them, it was struck by a hurled object accompanied by a crash of shattered glass.

With *Sally*, Marilyn Miller became the undisputed Queen of American Musical Comedy, her following practically a cult. The costume problem was apparently adjusted. Ziegfeld even provided a brand new one each night. He had her dressing-room done over by Sloan Farley in satin with velvet trimmings.

One day Billie returned home to find Burkely Crest swarming with reporters. Marilyn had given an interview in which she said she was forced to barricade her dressing-room to keep Ziegfeld out. She claimed that he was desperately in love with her and would marry her if Billie stepped aside. She added that all that held him was Patricia. 'She waves that child at him like George M. Cohan waves the flag.'

'It's a smart line,' remarked Billie, 'but I doubt she thought it up herself.' Billie did not step aside and, ironically, as with Olive Thomas, it was Jack Pickford who came to the rescue. Jack and Marilyn were married in late July of 1923 at Pickfair, the estate of Mary and Douglas Fairbanks, amid unparalleled rejoicing. Extra police were called, sight-seeing buses clogged the roads, and a number of people were apprehended scaling the garden walls. At the exact moment Jack and Marilyn were joined together, a plane swooped low and dropped orchids on the entire bridal party. They were not divorced until 1927.

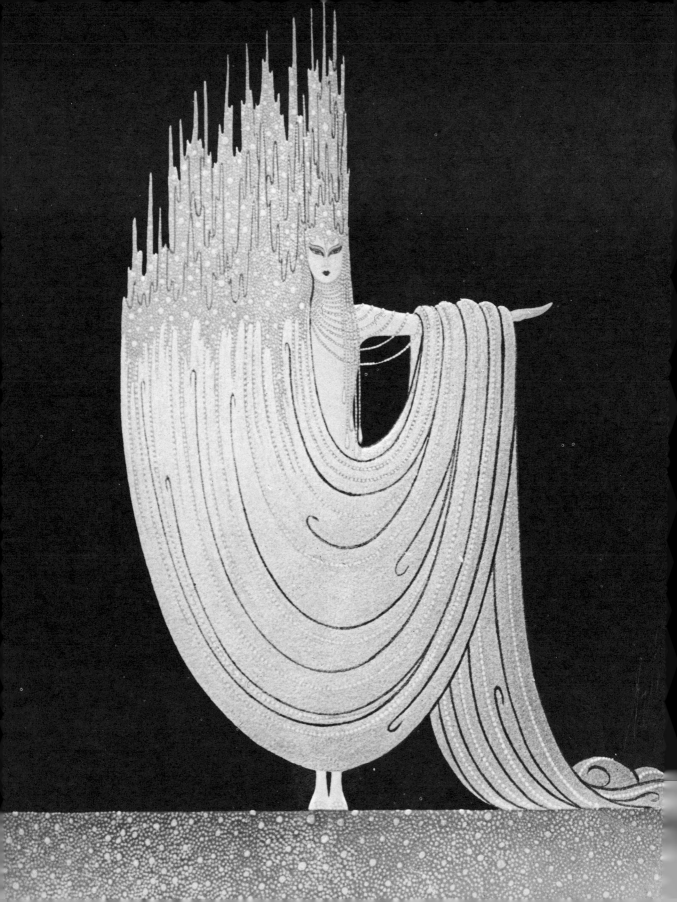

5

The Great Ziegfeld at Home and Abroad

IN A TRIBUTE TO ZIEGFELD, THE NOTED CRITIC, GILBERT Seldes, once wrote: 'He has sent genius whistling down the wind to the vaudeville stage and built up new success with secondary material; the store houses are littered with the gaudy monuments of his imitators.' The statement is not altogether true. Some of Ziegfeld's imitators were notably successful and even became serious competitors: *George White's Scandals, Earl Carroll Vanities, The Music Box Revues, The Greenwich Village Follies,* and later from London, The Charles Cochran and André Charlot Revues.

The Greenwich Village Follies, which materialized down on Sheridan Square in 1919 under John Murray Anderson's inspired aegis, achieved its effects by stressing simplicity, wit and taste. Anderson gathered around him such budding Village artists as Reginald Marsh, W. T. Benda and Cleon

A design by the Russian artist Erté for *George White's Scandals* of 1928. *Courtesy Charles Spencer*

Throckmorton who were able to work magic even with
sprayed burlap. When the series opened, it was called
Greenwich Village Nights, but when six weeks later it moved
uptown to the Nora Bayes Theatre, it became *The Greenwich
Village Follies*. Ziegfeld, a jealous god, responded with legal
thunder, but to no avail, as another *Follies* had been on the
boards in 1906 before Ziegfeld started his own series. The
move was made during the Actor's Equity strike, and, being
non-Equity, Murray Anderson's new show had no competition, all other productions being closed. It ran for 232
performances.

The 1920 edition, which also opened in Greenwich Village,
was soon moved uptown to the Shubert Theatre on West 44th

102

Street. Bert Savoy, a brilliant female impersonator, after whom Mae West is rumored to have patterned her swaying walk and modulated leer—later he was unfortunately felled by a bolt of lightning while strolling on Long Beach—was sensational as The Torso in 'The Naked Truth,' and as Lady Nicotine in 'The Hell Hole.' 'Just Sweet Sixteen,' a sugary confection with showgirls as candles on a cake formed by a single satin skirt, also brought down the house. James Reynolds, a flamboyant young Irish designer, a discovery of Anderson's, scored heavily with his designs for 'Song of the Samovar' in fourteenth-century Russian mood and with 'The Golden Carnival' in Empire style. Ziegfeld was definitely alarmed by this production and retaliated by raiding the ranks of the showgirls, taking Helen Lee Worthing, Juliet Compton, Irene Marcellus and Mary Lewis (Mary went on to achieve success in opera). James Reynolds was also recruited, though he maintained his connection with the Greenwich Village shows.

The Greenwich Village Follies continued until 1928, but declined after 1924 when Anderson joined Sam Harris and Irving Berlin for *The Music Box Revues*. The Village *Follies* were chiefly noted for their talented designers including Howard Greer (later a top designer of *haute couture*), Herman Rosse, Charles Le Maire, Adrian, Micho Ito, W. T. Benda, Nicholas de Lipsky, Reginald Marsh, Cleon Throckmorton and Erté of Paris.

Cleon Throckmorton, Charles Le Maire and Herman Rosse all became important designers. Throckmorton, who established his own studio, designed and built over six hundred sets. He worked with enormous speed and precision and had an unerring instinct for capturing the intention of the playwright. *The Hairy Ape, In Abraham's Bosom, Porgy and Bess* and *Three's a Crowd* are among his more notable efforts. During the Twenties and Thirties, Charles Le Maire lavished feathers, beads and chiffon on countless stars and ladies of the chorus. ('They were all beautiful when I got through with them.') He designed for the *Scandals* and the *Vanities*, but Ziegfeld was his favorite producer. He eventually became chief designer for Twentieth Century Fox (he won an Oscar for *All About Eve*). In 1958 he wrote: 'Even now I have the

103

memory of Ziegfeld knowing more about feminine beauty than any other person I have ever worked for.' Herman Rosse, another Oscar winner (*King of Jazz*, 1930), whose style was sharply contemporary and shot with brilliant colors, also designed many notable Broadway productions including *The Swan, Casanova*, and *The Emperor Jones*. The exquisite masks of W. T. Benda had a tremendous vogue throughout the Twenties. First seen in *The Greenwich Village Follies* of 1920, Charles Cochran featured them in London the following year in his revue, *The League of Nations*. Adrian, of course, went to Hollywood where, as top designer at Metro-Goldwyn-Mayer, he exerted a powerful influence on women's fashions the world over. Unfortunately for theatre, Reginald Marsh, probably the finest artist of them all, turned exclusively to painting where his exuberant and colorful delineation of life in Greenwich Village, the Bowery and Coney Island won him the title of the Hogarth of New York.

Erté's dazzling creations were also first displayed in the Village *Follies*. For the 1922 edition, Erté, who was a regular cover artist for *Harper's Bazaar,* did a stunning series of contemporary gowns, generously festooned with ropes of pearls, against a background of *Bazaar* cover designs. And the following season his fabulous 'Maid of Gold' costumes created a sensation in the *Ziegfeld Follies*.

The Music Box Revues (1921–1924) were stunning productions, built around and buoyed-up by Irving Berlin's exuberant scores. (Since his first successful song in 1911, 'Alexander's Ragtime Band,' which popularized ragtime throughout the U.S. if not the world, Berlin's music had continued to give new direction to popular song, away from set formulas and toward greater freshness and originality.) *The Music Box Revues* introduced the popular comedy team, Clark and McCullough, also Robert Benchley. All manner of tricky stage effects were employed. In 'Pack Up Your Sins,' the entire cast, including Gilda Gray and Ted Lewis, descended into Hell amid jets of steam and shooting flames. In 'Crinoline Days' Grace La Rue rose slowly from a trap, her hoop-skirt expanding until it finally engulfed the entire stage (an effect recently employed by Tom O'Horgan in celebration of Our Saviour in *Jesus Christ Superstar*). On the whole, however, the

Music Box Revues were more concerned with glorifying Berlin's songs than attempting to challenge Ziegfeld's eminence.

Earl Carroll, though he came late (1923), presented a more immediate threat. His Credo read:

EARL CARROLL VANITIES
A Mecca of Beauty

Appearance of a girl in the *Earl Carroll Vanities* entails being billed as 'One of The Most Beautiful Girls in The World.' After the ordeal of an Earl Carroll audition a girl feels, it is almost certain, that she is going to pass the most careful inspection by any other beauty expert in almost the entire world. Audiences invariably gasp at the First Full View of the Vanities' girls. They frequently express wonder at how and where Earl Carroll finds all the perfect types of feminine charm. Despite the fact that Mr. Carroll views nearly ten thousand applicants prior to every production, he exercises the same care with each individual. His eyes sparkle and his enthusiasm warms when he sees a new specimen nearer to perfection, just as does the lapidary or precious stone collector when he discovers a new gem. All girls with stage aspirations known that entrance into the *Vanities* spells success. *Earl Carroll Vanities* is the Mecca of Beauties from all Quarters of the Globe.

The Carroll-Ziegfeld Battle of Beauties provided plenty of copy for the press. Though Carroll's 'Living Curtains,' 'Virgins in Cellophane,' (draped nudity) and 'Horns of Plenty' never really cut very deeply into Ziegfeld's monopoly on beauty, Ziegfeld began a campaign to form an Alliance to Reform The Stage with the slogan, 'Back From Nudity to Artistry.' Ziegfeld announced his intentions of keeping the *Follies* 'as sweet and pure as he had discovered his audiences to be.' He wired New York District Attorney Benton:

I HOPE YOU WILL INVESTIGATE THE REVUES NOW PLAYING IN NEW YORK. NOT ONE OF THEM WOULD BE TOLERATED IN BOSTON OR PHILADELPHIA. THE BARING OF BREASTS OF THE YOUTH OF AMERICA TO DRAW A FEW EXTRA DOLLARS AND ABSOLUTE NUDE FIGURES DANCING AROUND THE STAGE SHOULD BE STOPPED BOTH IN THE REVUE AND THE NIGHTCLUBS. . . .

Sceptics, who recalled that Ziegfeld himself had introduced

A design by the Russian artist Erté
for the Ziegfeld Follies, 1923.
Metropolitan Museum of Art

RIGHT: Urban's Venetian scene for
the 1921 *Follies. Columbia
University Collection*

the bared breast, dubbed the campaign a 'Commercialization of Virtue.'

In 1926 Carroll threw a birthday party on stage for Mr. William R. Edrington, a Texas tycoon and one of his principal, backers. Since Edrington's birthday fell on the same day as Washington's, a gigantic portrait labeled 'The Father of Our Country' formed a benevolent background while an enormous tub of champagne occupied center stage. (It was later reported to be two inches of Sherry laced with ginger ale.) As everyone gathered about in festive mood, a showgirl, Joyce Hawley, stepped in, at which point the Federal Agents stepped out, charging Carroll with violation of the Volstead Act (Prohibition was in full flower) with the result that he was sentenced to one year and a day in the Federal Penitentiary at Atlanta, Georgia. Carroll was freed after serving four months and eleven days.

In recompense, perhaps, Edrington, at the cost of over four million dollars, built Carroll a theatre on Broadway and 50th Street with black velvet walls, chromium tubing, and reading lamps on the back of the seats. In spite of these innovations and the importation of elements of the London *Charlot's Revues*, including Noel Grey, Roland Leigh, Richard Addinsell, Anton Dolin and Jesse Matthews, the *Vanities* failed to prosper. Earl Carroll's garish theatre was demolished to make way for a Whelan's Drugstore, and Carroll himself perished in a plane crash with one of his beauties, Beryl Wallace.

Perhaps the most challenging of Ziegfeld's imitators was George White. Gene Buck had lured White, a dancer of considerable skill, away from J. J. Shubert's *Passing Show of 1915* and teamed him with Ann Pennington in the *Follies*. When in 1919 White opened his own revue, the *Scandals,* he lured Ann Pennington from Ziegfeld with the promise of better material and billing. Irked by the treachery of his former employee, Ziegfeld wired White that he would pay him two thousand dollars per week to return with Ann to the *Follies*. White wired back that he would pay Ziegfeld and Billie Burke three thousand dollars to go into his next *Scandals*. It marked the end of their professional association (though Ann Pennington was later forgiven) and the beginning of an extended and bitter feud.

Ziegfeld was one of the first American producers to import

ABOVE: 'Arabian Nights' curtain by Urban, executed in 1927. *Both from Columbia University Collection*

BELOW: 'Road to the Inn'. Urban's flower-strewn set for a scene from the 1924 *Follies*

109

the brilliant spectacles of the Parisian music-halls. The channel for their dissemination was Max Weldy, the famous French costumier for the *Folies-Bergère* and other shows. In his book on the designer Erté, Charles Spencer quotes an article on Weldy in a 1928 *Paris Soir*, referring to commissions from all parts of the world, and 'a revue costing one hundred thousand dollars for the USA.' 'Costumes, decors, curtains,' it continues, 'are exported by Weldy to the Winter Garden, to Ziegfeld, to the Apollo Theatre, New York.'

Erté, the Russian-born illustrator and designer, was launched on Broadway by Weldy. Ziegfeld commissioned him for a number, 'Gold', for the 1923 *Follies*, the Schubert Brothers put on a lavish spectacle, *Woman and The Devil* at the Winter Garden, and the artist also contributed to the *Greenwich Village Follies*. These occasional items came to an end when Erté was put under contract by George White, whose *Scandals* gained enormous prestige through Erté's designs for his magnificently opulent productions.

In spite of occasional striking designs by such artists as Erté and Max Weldy, the *Scandals* made no attempt to rival the *Follies* in sumptuousness. White's productions were rightly celebrated for their music, which blanketed Broadway for a decade. George White had spotted George Gershwin when Gershwin was acting as rehearsal pianist for *Miss 1917*. Gershwin's fresh command of the jazz idiom caught on with critics and public alike, especially as played by Paul Whiteman's Band and sung by Winnie Lighter. DeSylva, Brown and Henderson joined the *Scandals* in 1925. (Gershwin quit to do his own shows when White refused to pay more than $125.00 per week.) The trio forged some smashing scores including such all-time hits as 'Birth of the Blues,' 'Black-Bottom' and 'Lucky Day.' Ziegfeld did not enjoy hearing music from *George White's Scandals*. On one occasion when the band at the Sixty Club struck up a medley from George White shows, Ziegfeld stalked out followed by his party. The music, however, played on and on.

The decade of the Twenties was unquestionably the great period of the Revue, and in London, Charles Cochran, André Charlot and Noel Coward were its most celebrated exponents. Cochran's stage career started on Broadway as actor and stage

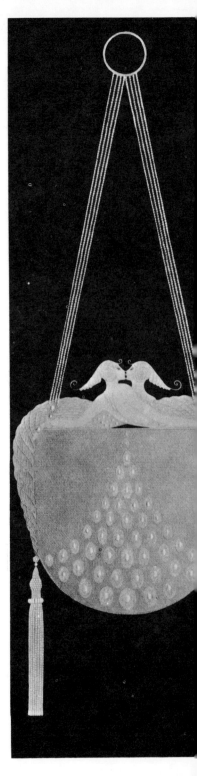

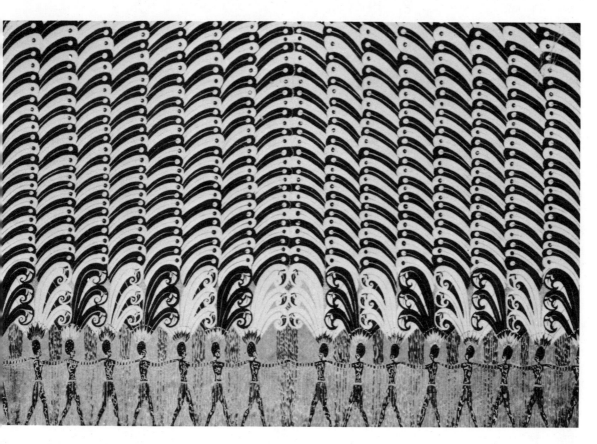

ABOVE: African Ballet curtain by
Erté for George White's *Scandals*
1926. *Courtesy Gunter Sachs, Paris*

LEFT: *The Handbag,* an Erté design
for the *Scandals. Courtesy
Gunter Sachs, Paris*

director at Niblo's Garden in 1892, and he later toured with
Joseph Jefferson in *Rip Van Winkle.* In London his activities
embraced many fields; everything he touched had style and
sophistication. His first major revue in 1920, *London, Paris and
New York,* introduced Irving Berlin to London, and this and
subsequent productions drew heavily on American talent. In
1921, *The League of Nations,* which was staged by John
Murray Anderson and designed by James Reynolds, contained
material from the early *Greenwich Village Follies.* 'The Nine
Most Beautiful Girls in New York,' four of them out of the
Ziegfeld Follies, and the Dolly Sisters, decked in feathers and
pearls by the celebrated Parisian designer, Paul Poiret,
supplied glamour. Irving Berlin, Gershwin and the then
unknown Cole Porter all had numbers in *Mayfair and
Montmartre* (1922), which was also staged by Anderson.
Florence Mills, another Broadway import, startled Londoners
with 'I'm Just Wild About Harry' from *Shuffle Along* and

'Dover Street To Dixie' from Lew Leslie's *Plantation Revue*.

In 1925 with *On With the Dance*, Cochran introduced his Young Ladies, his answer to Ziegfeld's Girls. The accent was on beauty and charm, but unlike Ziegfeld's beauties they were required to have sufficient individual talent to hold the spotlight for speciality numbers when required. Alice Delysia introduced Berlin's 'Pack Up Your Sins' from the second *Music Box Revue* and also sang Noel Coward's 'Poor Little Rich Girl.' Noel Coward, incidentally, turned over the lead in his play, *The Vortex*, to his understudy, John Gielgud, while he worked on *On With the Dance*, for which he supplied most of the material. *The Cochran Revue of 1926* was chiefly noted for introducing a brilliant new designer, Oliver Messel, but Hermione Baddeley and America's Elizabeth Hines also scored. Noel Coward's *This Year of Grace* was the Cochran blockbuster of 1928. It repeated its success in New York with such numbers as 'Dancy Little Lady,' 'Britannia Rules the Waves,' 'World Weary,' 'Arabesque'—danced by Tilly Losch—and 'A Room With A View'—sung by Jesse Matthews. *Wake Up and Dream* in 1929 was one of Cochran's loveliest revues with a superb score by Cole Porter which included, 'What Is This Thing Called Love,' 'I'm A Gigolo,' 'Looking At You' and 'Let's Do It.' It elevated Porter to the top rank of popular composers. Its success in London was repeated in New York.

The *Cochran Revues* flourished in London until 1942, long after the form had dwindled in New York. As a showman Cochran, though less flamboyant, was a worthy rival of Ziegfeld. His productions, whether musical or legitimate, were unfailingly distinguished. He surrounded himself with such illustrious designers as Oliver Messel, Rex Whistler, Cecil Beaton, Christian Berard, and Gladys Calthrop and fostered innumerable theatrical talents, composers, writers and performers, both British and American.

The *André Charlot Revues*, though more intimate than Cochran's, could hardly be described as modest. The settings were elaborate, there was an ample line-up of beautiful girls, but the emphasis was on writers and composers. Charlot gave Noel Coward his first London showcase in *London Calling* in 1923, but achieved his greatest success, at least in America, with the *First Charlot Revue* which starred Gertrude Lawrence,

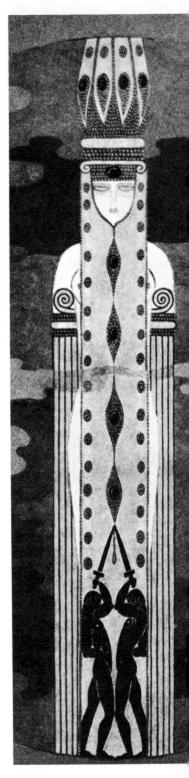

RIGHT: A design by Charles Le
Maire for the 1926 *Greenwich
Village Follies. N.Y. Public Library*

LEFT: One of Erté's designs for
the 1926 *Scandals*

Jack Buchanan and Beatrice Lillie, in reality a synthesis of his earlier London revues.

In Paris, where it all really started, the Folies Bergère and the Casino de Paris sparkled throughout the Twenties with Mistinguett (Ziegfeld imported her briefly), Fernandel, Jean Gabin, Josephine Baker and Maurice Chevalier. Chevalier's fame achieved international proportions, but neither in New York nor London did Josephine ever match her Parisian success. Only in her seventies, at Carnegie Hall, did she finally get a standing ovation in New York.

A design by Charles Le Maire for the 1926 *Greenwich Village Follies*. *N.Y. Public Library*

6

The Twenties—
Crest of the Wave

LIKE A SURFER, ZIEGFELD CAUGHT THE CREST OF THE WAVE of the Twenties, and maintaining a precarious balance, managed to ride out the turbulent decade in triumph. Considering the hazards of competition, coupled with his basically unstable nature and total lack of business acumen, it was a remarkable performance.

Flo was badly shaken by the Actors' Equity strike in 1919, a major upheaval which closed all the theatres in New York and on the road. He himself sought a court injunction to prevent the walkout, while the outraged Shuberts sued Equity for half a million dollars. The judge refused Ziegfeld's injunction; the Shuberts' case was thrown out of court. The Shuberts, whose abuses, along with those of Klaw and Erlanger, had been largely responsible for the strike, played both ends against the middle. Feeling the pinch with special sharpness because of their many empty theatres, they quietly forged a

final agreement with Equity. When Erlanger was appraised of the Shubert settlement he bellowed: 'Those sons-of-bitches—they sold us out!'

Ziegfeld's feud with Equity continued and erupted again in 1921 when his dismissal of a chorus girl, Elizabeth Chattern, was challenged. He called reporters to the Colonial Theatre in Chicago and announced:

> Nobody is going to tell me how to run a show. I put two hundred thousand dollars into a production and then Equity tells me how to run it. Not me! I've been paying about fifty thousand dollars a year to some actresses and actors. There are seven in the Chicago company who get one thousand dollars a week, and the actors have just no complaint against me. I don't want to fight them or their union. That's why I'm quitting. When producing is made a continual wrangle, then I want to get out.

Ziegfeld threatened to move his operations to London, but was ultimately forced to bow to Equity's demands, a bitter blow.

Erlanger's partner, Mark Klaw, had long been an unnecessary appendage. In 1920 Erlanger and Ziegfeld performed a clumsy amputation, eliminating Klaw's share of the *Follies* and *Frolics*. Klaw's reach, however, exceeded their grasp, and the resulting litigation dragged on for years. Ziegfeld's entire career was plagued with law suits and process servers. On his honeymoon he had been served with a writ by Harry B. Smith for $4,300 in unpaid royalties; and on 29 October 1929, while Wall Street crashed, he was in court contesting a bill of $1,600 from the Strauss Sign Company. His brokers being unable to reach him, this contest—which, incidentally, he did not win—proved extremely costly.

The problem of running his chaotic empire was eased by Matilda Golden, a remarkably efficient young woman who joined his staff in 1923. Bernard Sobel, Ziegfeld's publicity manager, has described her as 'black haired, bright-eyed and attractive, quiet, sympathetic and capable of holding all office activities in her mind at one time.' Goldie managed to bring order to his incredibly cluttered offices and somehow to cope with Flo's myriad and ever increasing eccentricities. She became in fact the final intermediary between the outer world and The Great Glorifier.

Harem scene by Urban for the 1919 Ziegfeld Follies. Columbia University Collection

117

William Randolph Hearst was undoubtedly the world's biggest spender, but Ziegfeld would easily have surpassed him had his resources been adequate. Always pressed for funds, even at times of greatest affluence, any creditor, no matter how trivial the sum, was anathema to him. When the wife of a coal merchant at Hastings appeared at his office to collect a sixteen dollar bill he told Goldie to 'get rid of her.' When Goldie protested, he snapped: 'Who are you working for? Me or the coalman?' In such cases Goldie would deftly juggle the books and Ziegfeld never knew the bill had been paid. Gretl Urban, who worked with her father on many productions, recalls frantic wrangles with Veronica, whose studio created many of the fabulous costumes, over her attempts to obtain them on credit in time for dress rehearsals.

In a *United News* release of 8 November 1923, Mrs. Clarence Brown, president of the Widows League of Chicago, complained:

118

Part of Urban's set for the 1915 *Follies. Columbia University Collection*

I let Miss Burke have my house to earn some money for our League. I was to receive $1,130 for two weeks. They talked me into paying the telephone bill and I have found that Miss Burke talked over long distance with everybody she ever knew—New York, Palm Beach, Hollywood, Westchester—no end. I left my twenty-two room house in perfect order and even had cut flowers in every room. Then they didn't pay the rent and I had to go after it and Mr. Ziegfeld wanted me to take $250 less than he had agreed to pay. He had the effrontery to say my house was filthy—my house!

Finally he wrote a cheque and on the back of it he wrote, 'Paid to a dishonest woman under protest.' Naturally I refused to accept it. It was an insult. I demanded cash. He telephoned to the box-office man and had him bring up $1,130 one dollar bills. It took me an hour to count it. It was all my chauffeur could do to carry it away. It just goes to show what we poor widows are up against. We must fight for everything.

It was Publicist Bernie Sobel who had to wrestle with Ziegfeld's bizarre publicity stunts; they included a cow-milking contest between Ann Pennington and Mae Dow, the tossing of a fake one-hundred-thousand-dollar necklace to shimmying Gilda Gray from a stage box by a 'Texas oil tycoon,' a showgirl dining with a pig at the Central Park Casino, a *Follies* party at Far Rockaway at which the girls danced in the surf under a full moon playing saxophones, a golf tournament at the Sand View Club with Shirley Vernon dressed only in a rain barrel—and the kidnapping of a performing ostrich.

Ziegfeld was notorious for his telegrams which he sent to all and sundry, sometimes to actors on stage when he himself was in the orchestra stalls, frequently to persons in neighbouring offices. Sobel was, of course, a prime target, sometimes receiving as many as twenty a day.

ALL I CAN GO BY IS WHAT I SEE IN THE PAPERS 20 YEARS I HAVE WORKED FOR THE AMERICAN ZIEGFELD GIRL AND NOW WHEN I HAVE THE MOST BEAUTIFUL OF ALL I HATE TO SEE THEM SIDETRACKED AND FORGOTTEN MAKE SURE GLADYS GLAD'S PICTURE IS IN EVERY PAPER WHEN SHE RETURNS I FEEL IF WHITE OR CARROLL EVER GOT HOLD OF A BEAUTY LIKE RUTH MORGAN THEY WOULD HAVE EXPLOITED HER LIKE I DID DELORES JUST LOOK IN MY OLD SCRAPBOOKS AND SEE HOW IT WAS DONE WHITE DOES SAME FOR SUSAN FLEMING SEND NOTICE OUT URBAN COMING UP HERE EXPLOIT HAZEL FORBES AND RUTH PATTERSON IS ALMOST FORGOTTEN SEE YOU SOON ABOUT GENERAL HAPPEINHEIMER AND HUNTING AND FISHING CLUB WAS NOT DRAMATIC NEWS WE PURCHASED 40 THOUSAND ACRES BUT NEW CLUB HAS ONLY 25 MEMBERS I AM PRESIDENT WILL WIRE WATSON HIS SUNDAY SHOWING WAS AWFUL ITS NOTHING PERSONAL YOU OR NO OTHER MAN CAN GET SEVEN HUNDRED DOLLARS WORTH WEEKLY IN PAPERS FOR ANY MANAGER THATS WHY MY PRESS DEPART-MENT COSTS PAPERS WONT PRINT THAT MUCH STUFF
REGARDS

When, on the brink of a breakdown, Sobel fled, he got a final telegram:

I FORGIVE YOU FOR LEAVING ME PERHAPS NEXT TIME YOUR WORD WILL BE GOOD I WILL BE GOOD I WILL TRY

Urban's setting for the Boston Opera's production of *Die Meistersinger* in 1912

TO DO ALL MY OWN PRESS WORK HEREAFTER AS I HAVE NOTHING TO DO AND SAVE 375 WEEKLY PLUS 50 DOLLARS FOR EACH SHOW IN ALL 525 WEEKLY THAT IS WHAT I HAVE ASKED KINGSTON TO PAY YOU I HOPE YOUR NERVES WILL SOON GET NORMAL AFTER YOU LEAVE ME I SUPPOSE YOU ARE EATING NOTHING BUT MATZOHS ALREADY PLEASE SEND ME SIX BOXES ON 6040 TRAIN TONIGHT GOOD LUCK MY POOR MISGUIDED BEST AGENT IN THE WORLD.

Ziegfeld bought an island in the Laurentian Lakes, twenty-five miles west of Quebec and christened it Billie Burke Island. For $150,000 he built a camp there which he named Patricia. It included a main house, a guest lodge, four cabins, a dormitory for the guides and another house built especially for Billie with a private boat-landing. The buildings, constructed of peeled logs, appeared rustic, but within they were luxuriously appointed. The staff included maids imported from Hastings, augmented by a couple of French-Canadian girls, a cook sent up from Dinty Moore's in New York, Dr. Wagner and a trained nurse, Blackie (in case of accidents), Patricia's tutor, Armond, eight native guides, gardeners and of course the cow.

Detail of Urban's set for the 1918 *Follies. Columbia University Collection*

121

Distinguished guests thronged throughout the summer and there were frequently as many as twenty at a table which groaned with broiled quail, salmon, trout and hot blueberry pies. Aileen Riggon, an Olympic champion who was summoned to teach Patricia to swim, departed twelve pounds heavier. Patricia recalls those summers and draws an affectionate picture of her father arriving tense, jumpy and tightly wound up, then slowly relaxing, cooking complicated dishes, stalking the woods, fishing, and growing a beard which he refused to shave off until called back to New York. These interludes were invariably brief. A note from Patricia offers a glimpse of life at the camp, and also conveys the affectionate tone of their relationship:

Dearest Daddy;

My, but a week has flown by and I meant to write you every other day. A lot has been going on and most of it has been fun. . . . We took lunch not as elaborate as when you're here but I made the fried tomato with the eggs on top and the cream corn with baked beans. We miss you very much aren't you coming up soon? We got seventeen trout and I am going to see if Mr. Rowly can send some to you. . . . The bears seem quite happy, Cracker loves to play with Dempsey but I am afraid he'll get hurt, then he can't go hunting with us. Bridget still sits in the water half the day, she doesn't bark at all, justs sits. Mummy is afraid she'll catch cold, but she won't stay out. The bears had colic last night and today they're on a diet of cinnamon and rice. Willie gave them too much sugar and water. He likes to see them stand on their hind legs and drink it out of a pop bottle. . . . We are going to make a movie but its going to be hard without any hero, Mummy said we can't have any of the guides as a hero, they are a bit old anyway, so I guess we'll have to make up Blackie or Miss Nick to be one. . . . How long do you think it will be before you will come up we miss you don't start another show right away. The mail boat is just docking and I'll give this to Emile. I drove it yesterday and docked it too, and I didn't hit a thing. I can't go out in my canoe by myself, won't you wire Mummy that it's all right. I'm just getting so I can paddle without changing sides. . . . All my love and kisses.

Patty

Winters in Florida were less idyllic, at least for Billie. Florida in the Twenties was experiencing a real estate boom, and

Flo Ziegfeld at the height of his career. *Romano Tozzi Collection*

Palm Beach was a Mecca for millionaires. Ziegfeld, of course, was in his element with deep-sea fishing, treasure hunts and a carnival of costume balls. They rented Colonel Bradley's Moorish palace which Billie tried to make homey by importing china, linens and glassware from Burkely Crest along with assorted animals from the Hastings menagerie. Home, however, was less appealing to Flo than Colonel Bradley's Gambling Casino where he might win, or more often lose, fifty thousand dollars at a sitting.

Billie did not take this excessive gambling lightly. She wept and stormed and threw things but, like an alcoholic, there was no reasoning with Flo about gambling. After one of their most outrageous scenes, Billie engaged a suite in a hotel in St. Augustine, assembled a mountain of luggage, Patricia and her household staff and prepared to leave Flo forever. He intercepted her at the front door.

'Good-bye,' said Billie 'I'm leaving you, Flo. I'm taking Baby with me, also Delia and Helen and Winifred, Alice and Jim.'

'I'm a sick man, Bill,' pleaded Flo. 'You can't do this . . .' Billie moved relentlessly out through the door and down the front stairs, trailed by her entourage. Flo overtook her on the bottom step. 'Five minutes—just give me five minutes alone with you, Bill.' They retreated into the house; presently Flo sauntered out alone. 'Everybody can go back to what they were doing before. The crisis is over.' He waved to Patricia, 'Your mother can't even run away from home without enough baggage for a world tour.'

In 1925, Paris Singer, who had finally despaired of Isadora Duncan when she refused his offer to purchase Madison Square Garden for her school, gave Ziegfeld *carte blanche* to create a new theatre at Palm Beach. Joseph Urban was summoned to transfer an old assembly hall north of the Everglades Club into a charming intimate playhouse christened Montmartre, with a sliding glass roof to accommodate the Florida sky and a real palm tree piercing the marquee. *The Palm Beach Girl*, which opened the theatre, was an enormous success with premiere tickets selling at two hundred dollars apiece. Irving Caesar, Rudolf Friml and Gene Buck wrote the lyrics, score and book. Morton Downey sang the chief vocal numbers, Claire Luce, fresh from Parisian triumphs, made her entrace from a

124

Flo discovered Fanny Brice in the Seamen's Transatlantic Burlesque. Her superb comic gifts carried her to the top. Here she stars in United Artists' *Be Yourself*, made in 1930. *N.Y. Museum of Modern Art*

shimmering, mirrored egg, and the chorus included Susan Fleming, Louise Brooks and Paulette Goddard. After the Palm Beach season, the show was transferred to New York under the title *No Foolin'* where, in spite of its opulence, it failed to create much of a stir.

The *Follies* are generally conceded to have reached their zenith in the 1921 and 1922 editions. In the former, Fanny Brice made history with 'Second Hand Rose' and 'My Man.' Ziegfeld himself had discovered Fanny in 1910 singing 'Sadie Salome' in the Seamen's Translantic Burlesque. Her superb comic gifts, her ribald sense of character and her essential beauty, which can best be expressed by the French term *belle-laide*, had made her one of Ziegfeld's greatest stars. The impact of her singing of the Parisian lament, 'Mon Homme' (originally intended for Mistinguett), was heightened by the audience's awareness of Fanny's personal tragedy. Her husband, the debonair gambler, Nicky Arnstein, who to Fanny 'stood for manners, education, good breeding and an extraordinary gift for dreaming' had dreamed himself into two years in Leavenworth Penitentiary for masterminding the theft of a million dollars in negotiable bonds from a bank messenger. The new dimension of Fanny's personality—the audience was too overcome to applaud—caused David Belasco to hail her as a second Duse. Unfortunately, Fanny never again displayed this facet of her extraordinary talent.

The *1922 Follies*, the costliest and most glittering, with a cast including Brice, Rogers, Fields, Mary Eaton, Mary Lewis, Gallagher and Shean, Gilda Gray and Evelyn Law, ballets by Michael Fokine, and the Tiller Girls from London, climaxed by Charles Le Maire's superbly costumed spectacle, 'Lace Land,' achieved theatrical apotheosis.

From this time on it is hardly surprising that succeeding *Follies* showed a sharp decline. Their erratic course was a more or less accurate reflection of the general chaos of Ziegfeld's private and business affairs. He was also losing irreplaceable stars. Bert Williams died suddenly in 1922. Fanny Brice checked out in 1923. Will Rogers left for the movies in 1924, and in 1925 W. C. Fields departed. Ziegfeld's reluctance to pay royalties, and his generally bad relations with composers, was hardly conducive to smash song hits, while both *George*

White's Scandals and *The Music Box Revues* were erupting with musical fireworks. By 1925 *The Follies* was very blurred indeed. And in 1926 due to legal snarls with Mark Klaw, there was no *Follies* for the first time since 1907.

Not that Ziegfeld was idle. He was, in fact, too busy with multiple projects to devote much time to the *Follies*. In 1922 he presented Billie Burke in Booth Tarkington's *Rose Briar*, and in 1924 in a musical comedy, *Annie Dear*, neither of which was an outstanding success. In 1924 he also produced a tepid

A strikingly unusual set by Urban, done in 1922, for a play that never saw the light of day. *Columbia University Collection.*

128

Detail of an Urban backcloth, complete with Flo's favourite emblem. It was used in the 1922 *Follies. Columbia University Collection*

operetta by Sigmund Romberg, *Louis XIV*, which was chiefly notable for Joseph Urban's incredibly lavish settings. In one scene a dining-table ran the length of the stage, appointed with the Russian Imperial banquet service which had so distressed Billie Burke when it was delivered to Burkely Crest. Food for the actors was prepared in the wings by a chef—but the show offered little sustenance to the audience.

Kid Boots, starring Eddie Cantor and Mary Eaton, compensated for these failures. Since the Equity strike of 1919 in which

Cantor took an aggressive stand against management, relations between Cantor and Ziegfeld had been strained, tensions in no way being relaxed by Cantor's subsequent appearances under the Shubert banner. But this smashing success brought them again into happy conjunction. Ziegfeld's interest in book shows, with their added lure of movie sales, had begun with *Sally* which was produced as a silent film for Coleen Moore in 1925, and again as a talkie with Marilyn Miller in 1929. *Kid Boots* also had an immediate movie sale.

Before the advent of sound, Ziegfeld's attitude toward film, like that of most Broadway producers, was faintly patronizing. His influence on films, however, was considerable. As early as 1916, D. W. Griffith had produced *Diane of the Follies*, in which for the first and last time, Lillian Gish was permitted to play a 'Wicked Woman.' The film has, alas, been lost; Miss Gish herself has no recollection of the plot beyond the luring of a socially prominent Long Island youth into her evil coils. In 1922 Constance Talmadge appeared as *Polly of the Follies*, in which an actor named Bernard Randall impersonated The Great Ziegfeld. The cast of *Pretty Ladies*, another *Follies* saga, (1925) included Ann Pennington, Zazu Pitts, Lilyan Tashman, Norma Shearer and Joan Crawford, and featured impersonations of Cantor, Rogers and Gallagher & Shean. In 1927, Billie Dove (in a moment of pique Louella Parsons dubbed her William Pidgeon), starred in *An Affair of the Follies*; and in 1928 *Phyllis of the Follies* featured Alice Day and Lilyan Tashman. Among film stars incubated in the *Follies* (besides Rogers, Cantor, Fields, Miller and Brice) were Olive Thomas, Mae Murray, Lilyan Tashman, Hazel Dawn, Billie Dove, Nita Naldi, Dorothy Mackaill, Ann Pennington, Mary Nolan, Virginia Bruce, Lina Basquette, Paulette Goddard, Louise Brooks and, of course, Marion Davies.

William Randolph Hearst was fifty-four when he plucked Marion Davies out of the 1917 *Follies*, thus initiating the most extravagant love story of the century. Marion Douras Davies, Brooklyn born (1897 or 1900) and convent bred at Hastings-on-Hudson, was the daughter of a New York petty politician, Bernard J. Douras. On 6 December 1918, Mayor Hylan, who frequently remonstrated, 'Mr. Hearst never asks me to do anything,' suddenly announced the

'My Rambler Rose'—song sheet from the 1922 *Follies* which starred the young Eddie Cantor. *Romano Tozzi Collection*

ABOVE RIGHT: A shot taken on the set of *When Knighthood was in Flower*. It starred Marion Davies (*center left*) and Alan Forrest. Urban stands behind director Robert G. Vignola. *N.Y. Museum of Modern Art*

RIGHT: Eddie Cantor as he appeared in Ziegfeld's smash-hit show *Kid Boots*, 1924. *N.Y. Public Library*

appointment of Bernard J. Douras as City Magistrate. The family moved to Riverside Drive, and Marion herself was sumptuously, if discreetly, installed in the Beaux Arts Apartments.

If Hearst, who had instigated the Spanish-American War single-handed, felt capable of turning Marion Davies into the greatest American movie star, no one can blame him. Marion was radiantly beautiful, talented, vital and charming. A brilliant light comedienne and a superb mimic, her impersonations of Lillian Gish, Pola Negri and Mae Murray in the hilarious comedy, *The Patsy* (1927), were devastating. Hearst, however, who guided her career with the same relentless hand that directed his empire, was determined to present her as a fairy tale princess of romance. He adored her in rich, period costumes surrounded by all the trappings of royalty. One can only guess as to the heights she might have risen had she not been weighed down by such spectacles as *When Knighthood Was In Flower, Yolanda* and *Janis Meredith*.

Hearst's interest in motion pictures antedated his meeting with Miss Davies. In 1915, motivated perhaps by his rich

131

land-holdings in Mexico which were threatened by Villa's revolutionary activities, Hearst began production of a fifteen-part 'patriotic' serial entitled, *Patria*. (This epic, incidentally, was the film Irene Castle was struggling to complete during the frantic rehearsals of *Miss 1917*.) Ever aware of

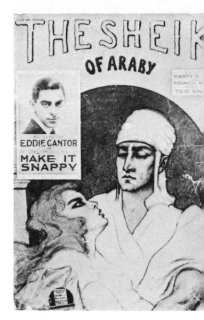

Song sheet of the Cantor number 'Sheik of Araby' in the highly successful Shubert musical *Make it Snappy*. *Heide-Gillman Collection*

RIGHT: Lillian Gish in the film *Diane of the Follies*. *Courtesy Lillian Gish*

LEFT: Marion Davies starred in the Hearst Cosmopolitan Productions super-spectacle *Buried Treasure* in 1922. *Columbia University Collection*

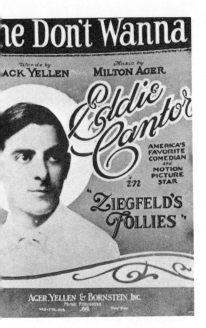

Song sheet featuring Eddie Cantor.
Heide-Gillman Collection

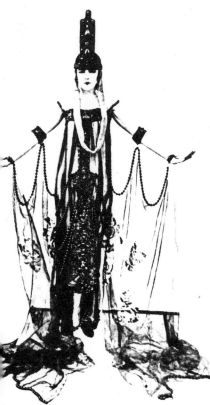

the Yellow Peril, the plot concerned a Mexican-Japanese conspiracy to overpower the US, with Warner Oland portraying a sinister Japanese baron, a characterization which Japanese Ambassador Hancihara found particularly offensive. *Patria* was so successful that President Wilson was prompted to write to Hearst International Films: 'May I say to you that the character of the story disturbed me very much. It is extremely unfair to the Japanese and I fear it is calculated to stir up a great deal of hostility. I take the liberty, therefore, of asking whether the company would not be willing to withdraw it.'

Patria was not withdrawn, nor did Pancho Villa's irregulars retreat. Hearst's Babicora Ranch in Chichieahua was looted of sixty thousand cattle and John C. Hayes, Hearst's manager, found it expedient to flee to El Paso. Outraged, Hearst's *New York Journal* demanded: 'Is it not time for the soldiers of the United States to do something PERMANENT? The way to IMPRESS the Mexicans is to REPRESS the Mexicans. The way to begin is to say to them: ''We are GOING INTO MEXICO. And as far as we GO, we'll stay''!' Fortunately this war never materialized.

The relationship between Ziegfeld and Hearst was always extremely cordial. In spite of Hearst's shyness, the two men obviously had much in common, though the majesty of Ziegfeld was necessarily of a smaller dimension. Hearst's two-hundred and twenty foot yacht, *Oneida*, which he kept staffed on the Hudson and only used occasionally, was regularly placed at Ziegfeld's disposal; and when Ziegfeld went to Hollywood in 1930 during the filming of *Whoopee*, the family was installed in Marion Davies' spacious villa (it contained 110 rooms and fifty-five bathrooms) beside the sea at Santa Monica. The two giants had a slight tussle over the services of Joseph Urban whom Hearst was anxious to engage for Marion's films. The matter was amicably settled when Hearst guaranteed not to allow Urban's work for him to interfere in anyway with the artist's commitments to the *Follies* and other Ziegfeld enterprises.

Joseph Urban, assisted by his daughter, Gretl, an artist in her own right, designed some twenty-five films for Hearst's Cosmopolitan Productions, including such Davies super-spectacles as *Buried Treasure, When Knighthood Was In Flower*

and *Yolanda*. Urban was not always happy with his film assignments, due to Hearst's imperious interference and the frequent gaps between inspiration and realization. His artistic direction, however, far surpassed most of the films of the day. Some of the less pretentious efforts, such as *Enchantment* (1920), a sentimental trifle with a Long Island setting, have enormous style and chic, the interiors anticipating the best of Twenties' design and the later Art Deco style of the Thirties.

Joseph Urban, a genial and charming man, was also a furious and concentrated worker. Between 1917 and 1933, as Artistic Director of the Metropolitan Opera, he designed most of the productions. His work there was described by Oliver Sayler in *Our American Theatre* as a process of awakening 'the somnolent Metropolitan from coma.' His magnificent plans for a new opera house did not, however, achieve the goal of moving the Metropolitan to 57th Street. The somewhat over-

Urban's baroque design for the Metropolitan Opera's *Cosi fan Tutte. Columbia University Collection*

ABOVE RIGHT AND BELOW: Loew's Paradise Theatre, Brooklyn; examples of the type of design Urban deplored. *N.Y. Public Library*

134

A corner of the St Regis roof garden, New York, showing Urban's enchanting mural, painted in 1927. *Columbia University Collection*

powering majesty of his design, widely debated at the time (1929), would seem, unfortunately, to have been echoed in some of the later excesses of Hitler's ace architect, Albert Speer.

'The growth of the modern opera orchestra,' Urban wrote, 'and the pageantry required for opera productions demand a more elastic stage and a larger orchestra pit. The auditorium, too, must change.' His plans for the Metropolitan included widening the stage to the full width of the auditorium which

Urban's set for the Marion Davies film *Enchantment*, 1920. His interiors anticipated the best of the Twenties and Thirties Art Deco style

prompted *The New York Times* to comment succinctly: 'A recent attempt to build a new opera house in New York had to be consigned to the scrap heap because Joseph Urban, in order to plan a rationally constructed auditorium, reduced the possible number of boxholders.'

When Loew's Theatrical Enterprises approached Urban with the proposition of building one of the cinema temples currently in vogue, Urban graciously refused. 'Every type of entertainment,' he observed, 'demands its own stage and auditorium. It is insane to witness a Charlie Chaplin comedy in an auditorium which represents a cross-breeding of the Vatican and Angkor Wat.' He did construct several quite suitable Spanish palaces for Florida millionaires, as well as a couple of fashionable club houses in that area. He also

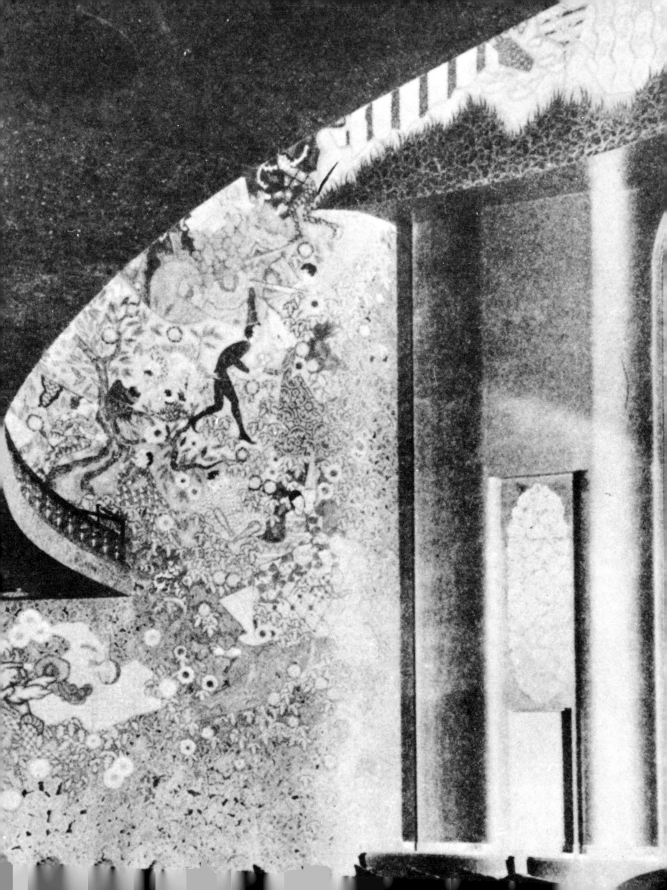

decorated restaurants and hotels in various cities, and several fashionable New York speak-easies.

Joseph Urban died suddenly on 10 July 1933 at the age of fifty-six. He had just completed an exhausting job as Director of Exterior Color for The Century of Progress Exhibition in Chicago. The stunning color and lighting effects which he did not live to see, served as a glittering memorial. As soon as the lights went out, however, his name lapsed into relative obscurity.

The May 1934 issue of *Architecture* contained articles on Joseph Urban by Otto Leegan and others, and *An Appreciation of Joseph Urban* by Harry and Janine Mahnken appeared in the *Educational Theatre Journal* of March, 1963. Both Yale University (1952) and the Library of Performing Arts at Lincoln Center in New York (1965) have had retrospective shows, but it is interesting to note that only a year after his death the comprehensive Exhibition of Theatre Art at the Museum of Modern Art in New York, contained no single example of Urban's work. In Lee Simonson's commemorative volume, *Theatre Art*, which celebrates the event in picture and story, there is only one passing reference to Urban, and that a line noting his flair for decoration. Perhaps the very range of his talents, reminiscent of the artists and craftsmen of the Renaissance, render his achievements suspect in today's era of specialization.

The New Amsterdam was a splendid theatre, but it was Abe Erlanger's and he never let Flo forget it. Abe had failed to mellow over the years, and his temper was not improved by the steady encroachment of the Shuberts upon his domain. True, he had abandoned his early habit of laying a loaded revolver on his desk, but one sensed that it still might be within reach. Ziegfeld was not only irked by Erlanger's omnipresence, but it was galling to know that Erlanger could benefit by his successes while enjoying virtual immunity from risk or failure. Occasionally Ziegfeld tried to beat him at his own game, even going so far as listing an assistant press agent as a chorus girl so that Erlanger might share the expense. It is doubtful, however, if such ploys fooled Abe, himself an

Urban's exquisite mural inside the Ziegfeld Theatre

139

expert juggler of books. The answer for Ziegfeld, obviously, was a theatre of his own.

Hearst owned considerable property on upper 6th Avenue and had just finished construction of the Warwick Hotel. Rockerfeller Center, of course, had not yet been conceived, and 6th Avenue (since renamed Avenue of The Americas) was a clutter of decaying buildings largely occupied by employment agencies. A handsome new theatre at 54th Street, opposite the Warwick Hotel, to be called The Ziegfeld, could hardly fail to boost property values, and Joseph Urban, who was the obvious man to build it, was approached around 1926. Urban was delighted to return to his first love, architecture. He designed, to use his own words, 'A modern playhouse for musical shows animated by gay detail to unite actor and audience.' The key note of the theatre was a muted brilliance. The stage, separated from the proscenium only by a perfectly plain wide arch, blended into the elliptical auditorium, the whole space without mouldings, smooth like the inside of an egg. The carpeting and seats were in gold tones which flowed up the walls to blend into a soaring mural composed of fleeting, romantic, slightly medieval figures, blurred in detail by subtle waves of color, a festive panoply enclosing the entire audience. The auditorium itself was softly illuminated from a central source, while the strong, modern decorative elements of the theatre's bowed facade were brilliantly lit to serve as a poster for the theatre.

In creating The Ziegfeld, Urban did not fail to include suitable accommodations for its maestro. A handsome suite of offices contained a private domain for Goldie, while for Ziegfeld himself he designed a chamber resembling a banqueting hall, large enough to accommodate a hundred guests. It was equipped with kitchenette, bath and a balcony which offered an unrestricted view of the entire auditorium. The area was beautifully furnished with antiques, and a massive refectory table was laden with silver cigar boxes, Tiffany vases and Ziegfeld's ever growing collection of good luck elephants, trunks erect, in silver, gold, porcelain and jade.

On 2 February 1927 the dazzling playhouse opened to a dazzled audience with *Rio Rita*, also designed by Joseph Urban, certainly one of Ziegfeld's most fantastic extravaganzas.

Rio Rita, 1927, was considered one of Flo's most successful—and extravagant—shows. *Heide-Gillman Collection*

140

Urban's setting for *Rio Rita*

OVERLEAF:
Façade of the splendid Ziegfeld
Theatre, built in 1926 and designed
by Urban. Compare this photo with
Urban's preliminary study on page
8. The theatre was pulled down in
1967 to make way for a skyscraper.
Columbia University Collection

As if all this were not triumph enough, the *1927 Follies*, which followed in the Spring, recaptured the old magic. Besides being the most costly to date ($289,035 prior to opening), it introduced Ruth Etting and marked the return of Eddie Cantor to the *Follies*. In 'It's Up To The Band,' the extravagant Busby Berkeley was anticipated by The Ingenues, nineteen young ladies at the keyboards of a battery of white baby grands. The Ingenues also played banjo, saxophone and other instruments, a harbinger of Phil Spitalny's All Girl Orchestra, and many similar bands to follow. To his other

141

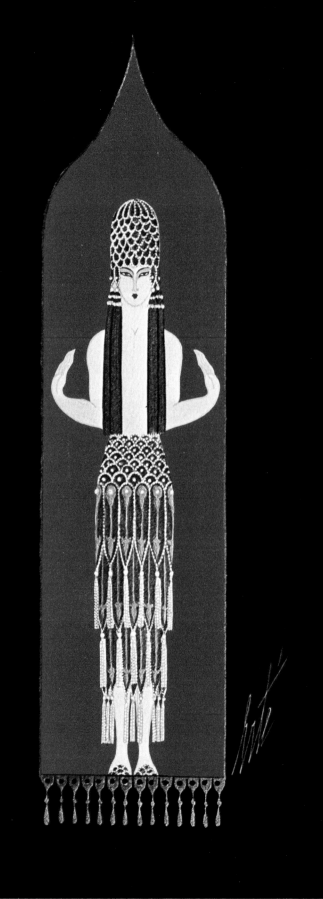

trademarks, 'A National Institution' and 'Glorifying the American Girl,' Ziegfeld added, 'He Who Glorifies Beauty Glorifies Truth.'

In 1926 Jerome Kern and Oscar Hammerstein had approached Ziegfeld about doing a musical based on Edna Ferber's best-selling novel, *Show Boat*. Discouraged by Irving Berlin who thought the notion preposterous, and disturbed by the sprawling character of the story with its overtones of miscegenation, Flo declined—until Kern's music won him over as it had Edna Ferber. 'The music mounted,' wrote Edna Ferber, 'and I give you my word my hair stood on end, the tears came to my eyes . . . That was music to outlast Jerome Kern's day and mine.' By 3 March 1927, when he sent a telegram to Kern, Ziegfeld was still undecided:

> I AM KEEN ON DOING SHOWBOAT ON ACCOUNT OF YOUR MUSIC BUT HAMMERSTEINS BOOK IN PRESENT SHAPE HAS NOT GOT A CHANCE IF HAMMERSTEIN WILL FIX THE BOOK I WANT TO DO IT OR ALLOW SOMEONE ELSE TO COME IN IF NECESSARY IF NOT YOU RETURN THE ADVANCE AS YOU YOURSELF SUGGESTED IF HAMMER-STEIN IS WILLING TO WORK WITH ME TO GET IT RIGHT LET'S DO IT TOGETHER ALL WE WANT IS SUCCESS . . .
> . . . ANSWER.

The answer was affirmative. Hammerstein's lyrics were superb, but Ziegfeld was never really satisfied with the book which he considered ponderous. In the light of recent revivals, it would seem that he may have been right. In any case, the fact remains that *Show Boat* marked the initial effort to make of musical comedy an integrated artistic creation, to fuse the disparate elements, song, dance, comedy and production numbers, so that each emerge naturally, even inevitably, from the play's context. Before *Show Boat*, plot, characters and setting had served merely as hooks on which to dangle song, dance and comedy routines. With *Show Boat* the dramatic text and musical score acquired scope and breadth, a concept which generated a long lineage, including such notable musicals as *On Your Toes, Pal Joey, Carousel, Oklahoma!, South Pacific, The King and I, West Side Story, My Fair Lady* and *Man of La Mancha*.

LEFT:
One of Erté's typical oriental figures designed for the Follies. *Private Collection*

PREVIOUS PAGE: Erté's design for 'The Golden Calf'. A scene from *George White's Scandals of 1926*

It is not to minimize Ziegfeld's contribution to *Show Boat* to note that he never had much faith in the show, and, in spite of ecstatic critical notices, was not convinced of its commercial potential until he saw queues form at the box-office. Ziegfeld gave *Show Boat* a superb production. He was responsible for the casting of Helen Morgan as Julie and the lovely Norma Terris as Magnolia. During the trial run in Washington, he cut, shaped and plyed his magic touch. However, Gretl Urban who worked on the production from its inception, recalls Hammerstein's relief that Ziegfeld seldom appeared at rehearsals, leaving matters entirely in Oscar's hands. Ziegfeld was responsible, against Hammerstein's better judgment, for the somewhat flashy finale (which undoubtedly contributed to the show's success), but by and large he ideally fulfilled the producer's function of allowing his creative artists full freedom to achieve their highest potential.

This happy state of affairs may have been due to the fact that Ziegfeld was also involved in the production of two other massive musicals, *Rosalie* and *The Three Musketeers*. *Show Boat* opened at the Ziegfeld Theatre on 27 December 1927; *Rosalie* went into the New Amsterdam on 10 January 1928, and two months later, after an extended out-of-town tryout, *The Three Musketeers* opened at the Lyric Theatre.

Some idea of the tone of *Rosalie*, an antiquated, romantic confection, is given by Alexander Woolcott's review in *The New York Times* of 11 January 1928:

> The sumptuous Florenz Ziegfeld, whose year this seems to be, emptied a great Horn of Plenty onto the stage of the New Amsterdam. First, down in the orchestra pit the violins chatter with excitement and brasses blare. The spotlight turns white with expectation. Fifty beautiful girls in simple peasant costumes of satin and chiffon rush pell-mell onto the stage, all squealing simple peasant outcries of 'Here she comes!' Fifty hussars in fatigue uniforms of ivory white and tomato bisque march on in columns of fours and kneel to express an emotion too powerful for words. The lights focus on the flowered gateway upstage, the house holds its breath, and on walks Marilyn Miller. . . . Though concocted by many hands, *Rosalie* is largely a collaboration between Sigmund Romberg and George Gershwin, which makes me think we may soon have a novel written by Harold Bell Wright and Ernest Hemingway.

Program cover for *The Three Musketeers*, a massive Ziegfeld musical of 1927, featuring Denis King. *N.Y. Public Library*

146

A powerful Urban backdrop for the
1927 *Follies. Columbia University
Collection*

There are many lyrics, some good, some fair. I am not sure who wrote them, but I feel reasonably safe in absolving Ira Gershwin of the one which contains the couplet:

> Though today its music
> Makes me'n you sick.

In spite of Woollcott, and largely due to the lure of Marilyn Miller, *Rosalie* was a hit. *The Three Musketeers* fared little better at Woolcott's hands, but audiences were enthralled by Dennis King, Vivienne Segal, Jack Harkrider's lavish costumes and Rudolf Friml's score. In congratulation, Percy Hammond of the *New York Herald Tribune* wrote:

Mr. Ziegfeld has, to his surprise, discovered that virtue is man's most lucrative occupation. Although he prospered in the days of his iniquity, his intake from naughty shows was nothing to that which now fills his purse to overflowing. I used to protest to Mr. Ziegfeld that his performances were harmful. 'Trust,' I pleaded, 'in the fundamental purity of the American drama lover. Give him and her,' I said, 'all the fluid shanks and shoulders that the police department will allow. Let them wanton a little among the contours and white surfaces of sex from the safe distance of the auditorium, but preserve us from contact with the sordid jokes of gutter librettos.' His enterprises were swamp lillies of the theatre, beauty arising from stagnant pools. But all of a sudden he has changed, ventured into fields more healthful, with the result that he is now the happy maestro of four pure and undefiled successes, *Rio Rita, Rosalie, Show Boat* and *The Three Musketeers*.

Song sheet for the musical *Whoopee*, a 1928 production by Ziegfeld. *Heide-Gillman Collection*

In the fall of 1928 Ziegfeld rounded out the fantastic year with *Whoopee*, another resounding success. Eddie Cantor starred and Ruth Etting, who took over from Ruby Keeler who went to Hollywood, was firmly launched on her brief but brilliant career.

And Ziegfeld's own career now truly reached its zenith. Free of the baleful Erlanger, secure in his beautiful new offices in his own splendid theatre, supported by a loyal staff and with three gold telephones at hand, Ziegfeld felt he could well afford dropping a hundred thousand dollars in a single night at the gaming tables. He also began to gamble heavily on the stock market.

Billie Burke gave a marvelous party, really a pageant, with eight groups of friends costumed to represent the casts of eight Ziegfeld shows, *The Follies, Kid Boots, Sally, Rosalie, Whoopee, Show Boat, The Three Musketeers* and *Rio Rita*. 'Everyone had fistfuls of money to spend,' Billie recalled, 'the world was a place created just for fun, and Flo Ziegfeld of all people was the man best equipped for having that fun. There was nothing to remind us that in China millions were struggling for a handful of rice or that in Japan, Russia and Germany mass man was responding to dangerous new ideologies. We would not have believed it anyway.' The Roaring Twenties, speeding on a collision course, were sheer delight.

7
Ebb Tide

On 29 OCTOBER 1929, THE STOCK MARKET CRASHED. SHOCK waves were felt around the world. Huge fortunes and life-time savings vanished over night; people in all walks of life found themselves suddenly penniless. There had been financial panics before, but nothing approaching such a holocaust. Quite a lot of people added to the confusion by jumping out of windows and committing suicide by other more conservative means. Such impetuous spirits sought a quick solution; but it took a painful decade and a world war to restore any semblance of economic stability.

That summer a gambler's hunch had prompted Ziegfeld to send a telegram from Camp Patricia to his brokers telling them to sell, but he was persuaded to counter the order by a close friend and associate, Paul Black, himself flying high in the booming market. The two went fishing and returned with a good catch, but on 29 October, when Ziegfeld emerged from his day in court with the Strauss Sign Co., he found he had lost everything—more than a million dollars.

Billie Burke was occupied with preparations for a Halloween party when Flo came home in a state of shock. 'Well, poor old darling,' she inquired, 'What is it?' 'I'm through,' he said, and gave way to strangled sobs. Billie threw in five hundred thousand dollars (saved out of her own earnings) to ward off financial disaster, though the family continued to travel by private railroad car with an entourage of maids, chauffeur, nurse, tutor, valet and several dogs.

And Ziegfeld, it turned out, was not yet through. By February of 1930 he had collected enough money from previous backers to produce *Simple Simon*, starring Ed Wynn. The book by Guy Bolton was weak, and Flo was so dissatisfied with Rodgers' score and Hart's lyrics that he refused to pay royalties. In the spring he went to Hollywood to supervise the filming of *Whoopee* for Samuel Goldwyn at Metro, another depressing experience. Only in the dance sequences was he permitted any authority. The young choreographer, Busby Berkeley, later to play such a prominent role in shaping Hollywood musicals, worked closely with Ziegfeld and successfully adapted many of Flo's concepts. The film treatment was heavy-handed, however, and lacked the high style and verve of the Broadway production.

Ziegfeld placed great hopes in *Smiles*, in which Fred and Adele Astaire appeared as society swells and Marilyn Miller again essayed the role of a forlorn waif, in this instance emerging as a Salvation Army lass. Marilyn's elfin magic was beginning to fade, and she suffered from recurring bouts of sinus infection which had plagued her for years and was to end her life in 1936. Rehearsals were chaotic. Ziegfeld quarreled with Vincent Youmans who had to be restrained by court order from withdrawing his music. A battery of writers, including Ring Lardner, was called in to bolster the frail book. The show was delayed for two weeks, but finally opened at the Ziegfeld Theatre on 18 November 1930 to an unusually brilliant audience. There were few smiles, however, and even fewer laughs. When *Smiles* closed it was three hundred thousand dollars in the red—and Flo was a sick man.

The one bright spot that winter was Billie Burke's success in

Comedian Ed Wynn starred in the unsuccessful musical *Simple Simon*, 1930—Ziegfeld's first show after the Wall Street crash in which he lost millions. *N.Y. Public Library*

Ivor Novello's comedy, *The Truth Game*, which Lee Shubert presented at the Ethel Barrymore Theatre. Lee Shubert, like everyone else, was enchanted with Billie. (The association was destined to prove fortuitous for them both.)

Abe Erlanger's far flung empire which had been steadily shrinking under Shubert pressure, was completely obliterated by the Wall Street holocaust. When, a broken man, he was asked why, with the power he possessed, he had ever permitted the Shuberts to gain their stranglehold, he replied, 'They're Jews, and I would never hurt a Jew,' a canon to which the Shuberts obviously did not subscribe. Erlanger died in 1930. He was given a rousing funeral, and immediately consigned to oblivion.

As the Depression deepened, the Shuberts also found themselves in deep trouble. In his definitive biography, *The Brothers Shubert*, Jerry Stagg describes the interview in 1933 during

151

which their lawyer, Willie Klein, begged Lee and J.J. to liquidate their holdings and clear out. 'You can live like kings, travel, go anywhere you want. Who wants empty theatres? Who needs them! Tear down the theatres and go for office rentals.'

J.J. was immediately on his feet, his voice trembling. 'What the hell do you know? I tell you, when you tear down a theatre, it's like a death in the family.'

'Do you think we did it all just for money, Willie?' asked Lee, not looking at his brother. 'Just for silly money! I'm not ashamed of the money we made. I'm not ashamed of the name Shubert on theatres. It makes me very proud. But we did not come to New York to work and let our work die.'

In spite of the bitter rivalry between them, the brothers

Eleanor Powell starred in the spectacular 1936 film version of *Rosalie*, Flo's earlier musical.

Bert Lahr, the comedian, in *Hot-Cha*, made in 1931. One of Ziegfeld's last shows, it was a flop, in spite of the volatile Lupe Velez. *N.Y. Public Library*

stood together in this crisis. They had to dip into their Swiss bank accounts. Eventually the gesture paid off handsomely (they were able to pick up numerous blocks of Midtown real-estate dirt cheap), but the fact remains that single-handed they kept the theatre alive through the Great Depression.

In the Spring of 1931, Burkely Crest was shuttered, the animals dispersed, the servants discharged. Billie and Patricia left for the West Coast where Billie had contracted to appear in Paul Osborn's hit comedy, *The Vinegar Tree*. 'It's all going to come out all right,' said Flo when they parted in Chicago. 'I'm going to do another *Follies* and everything will be fine.'

On 16 June he wired from Pittsburgh where the *Follies* were trying out:

ARRIVED WITH TWO HUNDRED AND TWO PEOPLE HOW I MANAGED IT IS A MIRACLE DARLING I'VE HAD ABOUT THREE HOURS SLEEP IN 48 HOURS BUT FROM FINAL REHEARSAL I THINK IT WILL PROBABLY BE WORTH IT TERRIFIC BIG SHOW BIGGER THAN ANY I HAVE EVER HAD IN MY ENTIRE CAREER MATERIAL LOOKS GOOD BUT YOU NEVER CAN TELL WHATS GOING TO HAPPEN . . .

The final *Follies* opened at the Ziegfeld on 21 July 1931. The score by Mack Gordon and Harry Revel contained no hit tunes. Ironically, the only show stopper was Ruth Etting's revival of Nora Bayes' 'Shine On Harvest Moon' (injected at the last moment) which had been Flo's first song hit back in 1908. In 'Changing of the Guards' the girls paraded in uniform before Buckingham Palace, and in 'Illusion in White,' against one of Urban's most spectacular settings, the Albertina Rasch dancers in Harkrider's chic tights swished dramatic ostrich feather trains. (John Harkrider was the last of the important fashion designers to glamorize the Ziegfeld Girls.) At the final curtain the company was enveloped in balloons and confetti. The show was big, but in 1931 it all seemed strangely irrelevant.

With the *Follies* limping along to half-filled houses, Ziegfeld was obliged to turn to Dutch Schultz, a picturesque underworld figure, to finance his next production, *Hot-Cha*, in which he hoped to recapture the success of *Rio Rita*. The aggravation of having mobsters hanging around during rehearsals was minor

153

compared to the tempestuous performance sustained by Lupe Velez who kept the company in a state of constant pandemonium. The critics raved about Charles Le Maire's costumes, but Lupe failed to rouse the audience and the show flopped. (Dutch Schultz's troubles were ended on the night of 23 October 1935 when he was cornered by Mendy the Bug in the gents' room of the Palace Chophouse in Newark and shot to death.)

During the brief run of *Hot-Cha*, it looked as though salvation might be at hand through an alliance between Flo and Samuel Goldwyn. The two were presumably to join hands on equal terms to produce films worthy of one another. However, Flo gave instructions that his name was to be given

The finale of *Show Boat*, 1927. The magnificent Urban sets enhanced what was almost certainly Ziegfeld's greatest success

Stars from the *Show Boat* revival,
Paul Robeson and Dennis King

preference in all press releases and he was also to be credited with having originated and developed the entire plan. So for the first time in his career, Sam Goldwyn's name was slighted. He was deeply offended and the Ziegfeld-Goldwyn union perished in embryo.

After the failure of *Hot-Cha*, process servers became so numerous that Flo was frequently forced to flee by way of a fire escape and through the theatre cellars to the alley where his Rolls awaited. The office staff was completely demoralized, and the situation was further aggravated by Goldie's sudden marriage. Flo regarded the marriage as unforgiveable. To make matters worse, on the return from her honeymoon in Bermuda, Goldie suffered an attack of appendicitis and was rushed to hospital.

Though on the point of physical exhaustion, Ziegfeld somehow managed to summon the strength to produce a weekly radio series for Chrysler, hosting the program himself and using music, scenes and stars from his various productions. Rehearsals were arduous. Listening one night in Santa Monica, Billie heard his voice falter. 'It was only a little break, unnoticed by anyone else, but over three thousand miles I caught the weariness and sickness of it.' Billie canceled a new play she was rehearsing and headed East.

She was shocked to see how thin he had become. His neck was shrunken, his broad shoulders hunched, the elasticity of his walk gone. One evening when they went to the Pennsylvania Hotel to hear Buddy Rogers' Band, Flo collapsed and they had to take a room there for the night. Doctors recommended rest, but Flo had already embarked upon a revival of *Show Boat*. With Paul Robeson singing 'Old Man River' and Dennis King as the dashing river gambler Ravenal, the revival of *Show Boat* actually surpassed the original. Nevertheless, a casualty of the Depression, *Show Boat* failed to last out the long hot summer. In spite of its failure, Ziegfeld may be said to have passed from Broadway in a final blaze of glory.

In a flight from creditors and the pressures of New York, Billie took him to California. Pleurisy had set in. On the terrible trip west, Flo was incoherent much of the time. At Billie's bungalow in Santa Monica, in a room crowded with flowers, he rallied for a while, sending telegrams (six thousand dollars' worth) and making telephone calls, most of them about eighty dollars apiece. 'I know it's expensive, Baby,' he said to Billie, 'but I do love the telephone.' The pleurisy flared again and Flo was transferred to the Cedars of Lebanon Hospital.

Billie was working at RKO, playing the mother in *A Bill of Divorcement* with John Barrymore and a newcomer to films, Katharine Hepburn. On the afternoon of 22 July 1932, she was called from the set where she was making a test with another newcomer, Walter Pidgeon. She rushed to the hospital in full make-up and a long dinner dress, but Flo died moments before she arrived.

Billie and Patty were secluded in Will Rogers' home while Rogers arranged a quiet funeral. The service was only slightly marred by the minister who repeatedly referred to Ziegfeld as Zieg*field*, a solecism Flo particularly detested. In eulogy, Will Rogers wrote:

> He picked us from all walks of life and led us into what little fame we achieved . . . He brought beauty into the entertainment world. To have been the master amusement provider of your generation, surely a life's work has been accomplished. . . . He left something that hundreds of us will treasure till our final curtains fall, and that is a 'badge', a badge of which we are proud and want to read the lettering:
>
> 'I worked for Ziegfeld'

And in epitaph, Billie selected a quatrain from Shakespeare's *Venus and Adonis*:

> For him being dead, with him is
>   Beauty slain;
> And beauty dead, black chaos
>   Comes again.

There was, in fact, as much truth as poetry in the lines. After the obituaries, the press palpitated with stories of Ziegfeld's insolvency. It appeared that his debts amounted upwards of a million dollars and numerous creditor suits were immediately launched. Goldie remained at her post until representatives of the District Attorney's Office closed Ziegfeld's offices and siezed all documents in the files. Alice Pool stuck to her switchboard till the very last. The offices were empty, cabinets, waste-paper baskets, even the ink-wells, when the elevator boy admitted a reporter. Then Alice cracked, screaming invectives, cursing and finally collapsing in a shuddering heap. A locked safe was discovered in a remote closet. Reporters and police stood by as it was opened by the proper authorities. It contained eleven rubber bands, two five-dollar bills, three song copies, a large glass ruby, a silk whip with a rhinestone handle and a small bronze elephant.

In Hollywood Billie went back to work on *A Bill of Divorcement*. 'And so I began to do my silly women. Those characters, those bird-witted ladies whom I have characterized so often . . .' In 1948 she wrote:

> I am neatly typed today, of course, possibly irrevocably typed, although I sincerely hope not for I should like to do better parts. I could do better parts better . . . Now, of course, I know what I should have done. I should have returned to Broadway . . . I know that I could have found good plays and good producers, and I am reasonably sure that I could again have been a star on the New York Stage. But my immediate need was to make a little money and to look after my daughter. I did what I had to do at the moment . . .

Several months after Flo's death, Billie, floundering in a morass of debts, wrote to Lee Shubert asking him if he would consider reviving the *Ziegfeld Follies*. 'It would keep Flo's name alive.' And she added diplomatically, 'I trust you to do the show as you would have done it with Flo, if things had been different.'

The prospect of doing a *Ziegfeld Follies* tickled Lee's ego. He made a deal in which Billie was to receive one thousand dollars and three per cent of the gross profits. Lee then informed J.J. that this was his deal and that J.J. was to have nothing whatever to do with the show. J.J. who, because of his *Passing Shows*, considered himself the greatest living master of Revue, was publicly humiliated. If, due to the brothers' united stand on the matter of preserving their empire, there had been any chance of personal concord between them, it was now utterly dashed. For the next twenty years Lee and J.J. sat in their offices on opposite sides of West 44th Street without ever meeting, communication between them being conducted entirely through lawyers and other privileged intermediaries. J.J. did not even attend his brother's funeral which took place on 26 December 1953. He spent the day in his office looking over papers.

157

J.J. had never prayed harder for a Ziegfeld flop. He was bitterly disappointed when the 1933 post-Ziegfeld *Follies* (presented under the name of Mrs. Florenz Ziegfeld Jr. to lend authority) opened to rave reviews in J.J.'s own theatre, The Winter Garden, a success mainly due to John Murray Anderson who was called in at the last moment to pull the show together. It had an attractive score by Vernon Duke. The cast included prima-donna Jane Froman, funnymen Willie & Eugene Howard, new-comer Eve Arden, fifty girls in the line and Fanny Brice who did a take-off of Amie Semple McPherson, 'Soul Saving Sadie' and 'Sunshine Sarah' (. . . 'Oy—I'm a noodist'). The show also marked Fanny's first appearance as Baby Snooks.

The next edition (1936) was also worthy of Flo, with settings by Vincente Minnelli and costumes by Raul Pene Du Bois, a brilliant young designer whose creations brightened numerous productions in the ensuing decades, climaxed by his stunning transformation of Barnum and Bailey's Circus. The choreography by Robert Alton and George Balanchine foreshadowed their future triumphs in ballet and musical theatre. Bob Hope as Master of Ceremonies hosted such stars as Eve Arden, Gertrude Niesen, Josephine Baker (audiences liked her but the press didn't), Bobby Clark, Gypsy Rose Lee and Fanny Brice. It was to be Fanny's last show. She returned to Hollywood to concentrate on collecting modern painting and on interior decorating with an occasional sortie into films and radio.

If Ziegfeld's creditors had any illusions about benefiting from the post-Ziegfeld *Follies*, they didn't know Lee Shubert. In a complex deal involving the Ziegfeld and Erlanger estates, he had purchased all rights to the name, *Ziegfeld Follies*, for $27,500, a manoeuvre which really paid off when he sold them to MGM in 1945 for one hundred thousand dollars for the film, *Ziegfeld Follies*.

The Shuberts, though inconvenienced by the Depression, were not nearly so distressed as William Randolph Hearst. At first he had hoped that it would simply go away, but when it didn't, he presently discovered himself in debt to the sum of $126,000,000 and besieged not only by creditors and angry stock holders, but by US Treasury officials, who contended

MGM's lavish film *The Great Ziegfeld*, made in 1936, was 'based more on spirit than fact'. It starred William Powell and Fanny Brice; Luise Rainer played Anna Held

that Hearst had evaded two and a half million dollars in taxes for 1934 and two and three-quarter millions in 1935. He borrowed a million dollars from Cissy Patterson at five per cent and Marion Davies threw in another million which she had saved. Hearst cut his own salary from five hundred thousand to one hundred thousand dollars. He had been endeavoring to sell the Ritz Towers which was appraised at six million, but when the bank took it over, Hearst and Marion were evicted from their New York home. (Hearst and Marion eventually settled in Wyntoon, a Bavarian village Hearst had constructed on the McCloud River in Northern California and

159

which Marion detested and dubbed 'Spittoon'.) He also sold six radio stations and numerous newspapers, but he was unsuccessful in disposing of a Spanish cloister which had been crated, stone by stone, into the country and stored in a Bronx warehouse. Boys' clothing and infants' wear were

An impression of Coney Island: Reginald Marsh's painting, *Pip and Flip, Twins from Peru*, was painted in 1932. *N.Y. Gallery of Modern Art*

removed from the fifth floor of Gimbel's Department Store and about a third of Hearst's fifty-million dollar collection of art objects was crammed into the two-acre space to be sold on the store's Easy Payment Plan. In the midst of all this ferment, Hearst was grateful to Loew's Theatrical Enterprises which was operating the Ziegfeld Theatre (which had reverted to Hearst) as a motion picture house. Loew's Enterprises, incidentally, had every intention of eventually acquiring the property.

Billy Rose also had an eye on the Ziegfeld Theatre, particularly on Ziegfeld's suite of offices which he had visited, but where he had never been received. Billy Rose was a wheeler-dealer par excellence, and the best deal he ever made was marrying Fanny Brice. Fanny was never able to explain to herself or to anybody else how it happened. She met him in a speak-easy when she was thirty-six and Billie was twenty-nine. Fanny had recently divorced her great love, Nicky Arnstein, who, once out of jail, started running around with other women. If it was on the rebound, Fanny certainly collided with an immovable object. Nothing fazed Billy. They were married on 9 February 1929 in City Hall by Mayor Walker. Billy moved into Fanny's swank apartment on East 69th Street where he met all the theatre greats and appropriated most of them. After their marriage Fanny left the *Follies* and turned a tawdry revue, *Crazy Quilt*, which Billy Rose produced, into a long run hit. She also put over his Casino de Paris, a flashy night club which he operated at Depression prices in the Earl Carroll Theatre. Billy didn't even mind being called Mr. Brice until he made his second million, at which point he shed Fanny for Eleanor Holm, an Olympic swimming star and a champion out of the pool as well as in.

By a masterly stratagem, in itself worthy of a chapter, Billy Rose managed to snatch the Ziegfeld Theatre from under the very nose of Loew's Theatrical Enterprises, though he would never have been able to pull it off had old Marcus Loew not been dead and buried. He obtained the magnificent structure for the paltry sum of $630,000. Billy Rose did have an appreciation of art, whether for art's sake or for his own, and he was determined to restore the Ziegfeld to its former elegance which had been considerably ravaged by untidy movie

161

audiences. He called in Gretl Urban (since her father's death she had been managing his studio) to oversee the renovations. Miss Urban was relieved when he received her in Ziegfeld's old offices in his pajamas, a refinement he was rumored frequently to omit. She was also delighted to hear that he intended to restore the theatre in every particular, altering no element of her father's design. This was done, and though the house was never very profitable (it was too large for legitimate plays and not large enough for musicals with rising production costs), Billy Rose maintained America's most beautiful theatre, Urban's and Ziegfeld's monument, as his own private preserve until his death. One day Fanny Brice and Rowland Leigh, British lyricist and screen-writer, were passing the Ziegfeld Theatre. Fanny paused, looked toward the windows of Flo's office suite, now Billy's domain, and remarked: 'Up there sits the most evil man I have ever known.'

The property was sold by Rose's estate for eighteen million dollars. In the *World Journal Tribune*, Sunday 19 March 1967, the following appeared:

A STONE FOR THE ZIEGFELD

The Ziegfeld Theatre, or what is left of it, is due for one last show next month. There will be ceremonies when the demolition crew gets down to the corner stone. Patricia Ziegfeld, daughter of the late illustrious impresario, will fly in from Los Angeles. She is now Mrs. William Stephenson, married to a California architect. The memorabilia contained in the corner stone will be presented to the Smithsonian Institute.

(On 26 July 1926, Patricia herself had cemented the corner stone which contained, among other mementos, photographs of Ziegfeld's mother, Billie and Patricia, a program of *Sally*, a program of the first *Follies* in 1907 and a brick from an ancient Greek theatre. She must have found the opening a somewhat traumatic experience.)

Incidentally, the two enormous reclining figures above the Ziegfeld entrance have already been claimed by souvenir hunters. One entire figure, weighing a ton, will go to the East Hampton estate of theatre angel, Evan Frankal. The head of the second statue is earmarked for the Sutton Place Terrace of Zachary Fisher who is building the new skyscraper on the site.

Two stills from MGM's *The Great Ziegfeld*, 1936

ABOVE: William Powell as Ziegfeld

BELOW: Replica of a street scene from the first *Follies* of 1907 *M.G.M.*

Still from the film *Rosalie*. M.G.M.

Fisher's skyscraper was duly constructed, and behind it a new movie house, optimistically christened The Ziegfeld. It has splendid retiring rooms and lobby to match, heavily festooned with crystal chandeliers which appear suspiciously plastic. Bits and pieces of Ziegfeld memorabilia haunt the lobby and mezzanine, but the theatre proper resembles a glorified bowling alley.

When Metro produced *The Great Ziegfeld* in 1936, they acknowledged that the film was based 'more on spirit than fact.' William Powell was credible as Ziegfeld; Luise Rainer also managed to make Anna Held believable (she even won an Oscar), but if the facts were fiction, the spirit was equally spurious. The production numbers were elaborate in the

164

Hollywood idiom, but made no pretense of capturing the delicacy and taste of the typical Ziegfeld show. Fanny Brice brought the film into brief focus, but unfortunately most of her rendition of 'My Man' landed on the cutting-room floor.

Ziegfeld, again portrayed by Powell, fared even worse in the *Ziegfeld Follies* (1945) in which he appeared in a prologue in a heaven created by designers Cedric Gibbons and Jack Martin Smith. It resembled a bridal suite in Miami's Fontainebleau Hotel, complete with plaster balcony and an expansive view of the firmament. The film itself was briefly enlivened by Fanny Brice in a sketch from the *Follies*, 'The Lottery Ticket,' and a couple of dances by Fred Astaire. Ziegfeld appeared once more (this time played by Walter Pidgeon) in the recent film biography of Fanny Brice, *Funny Girl*. The film was magnificently produced with great attention to period detail, but again Ziegfeld emerges as a bloodless figure. He fares better in *The Ziegfeld Girl* (1941) and *Till The Clouds Roll By* (1946), a truly stupefying biography of Jerome Kern. In both movies Ziegfeld is repeatedly alluded to, but never required to appear. Probably the best of the biographical films emerging from a *Follies* background is *Love Me or Leave Me* (1955) in which Doris Day gives an extremely effective performance as Ruth Etting while James Cagney is chilling as Ruth's husband and nemesis, the Gimp.

Ziegfeld's impact on musical films was tremendous throughout the Thirties and even into the Forties. Except for King Vidor's *Hallelujah* and Rouben Mamoulian's *Applause*, there is scarcely one of the scores produced that does not stem to some degree from Ziegfeld's concepts. Busby Berkeley evolved a bizarre style of his own in purely cinematic terms, but his basic concepts also sprang from *Follies* extravaganza. Other choreographers such as Sammy Lee and Roger Edens were similarly motivated.

In 1929 Ziegfeld himself had made an abortive attempt to produce a movie musical. *Glorifying The American Girl* never got very far off the ground and certainly into very few theatres, due largely to Paramount's ineffectual management which placed every obstacle in Ziegfeld's path. The film was shot at the Astoria Studios on Long Island with primitive sound equipment, but Mary Eaton is charming as the sales girl who goes to Broadway success in the *Follies*, and the production number which climaxes the film is stunning, suggesting that if Ziegfeld had had the opportunity to master the new medium, he might well have achieved considerable success in films.

But in the final analysis, the world of Flo Ziegfeld was the world of the theatre, and the world of the theatre, as a reflection of its own time, is necessarily ephemeral. The opulent period in which he lived, a world of wealth and naive fancy, is vividly mirrored in the extravagance of his life and work. Ziegfeld himself remains something of an enigma. He has been compared to Lorenzo the Magnificent and to a witch doctor presiding over tribal dances. Both are apt. The clear perspective which time should afford is something of an illusion. The prism of time may exhibit rainbow hues, but the

elements it discloses can never be accurately reassembled or
wholly resolved. To Patricia Stephenson, quietly reminiscing
on the terrace of a closed garden in Los Angeles, Flo is the very
paragon of a loving parent, gentle, humorous and affectionate.
To the Shuberts, Charles Frohman, George White, Earl
Carroll, Ring Lardner and other assorted enemies, he was
anathema. The Glorified Girls revered him, as well they might,
and women in general found him fascinating. In one of his rare
statements, Gene Buck observed: 'Flo could find little things
to do for women that would never occur to other men. He
understood better than anyone what it is that pleases women
most. He could flatter a woman by unusual attentions to a
greater degree than it would be possible for an ordinary man.

When he set out to win a woman, she could expect a period of glorifying surprises.' If the *Mémoires* of Anna Held are to be credited, he emerges as a monster. Eddie Cantor, in spite of their frequent rows, regarded him as a second father, and the devotion of Will Rogers and Fanny Brice is unquestioned. Noel Coward—with Archie Selwyn, Ziegfeld imported *Bitter Sweet* in 1929—regarded him with undisguised distaste, while Rodgers and Hart and George Gershwin found him intolerable. Lady Duff-Gordon—they certainly spoke the same language, though with different accents—considered him in all respects 'exemplary.' His staff, including Gene Buck, Bernard Sobel, Alice Pool and Goldie, were harried to the point of madness, but their loyalty was unswerving. To such cronies as William Brady, Hearst, Paris Singer, Colonel Bradley and assorted society figures, he was genial host and boon companion. Joseph Urban's position was unique in that Ziegfeld needed Urban more than Urban needed him. This delicate imbalance resulted in an unusually harmonious association. Gretl Urban was always treated by Flo with fatherly affection. As a detached observer, yet increasingly involved in the chaos of production, she never ceased to marvel at the blend of taste and vulgarity, the spectacle of genius at work. Doormen and cleaning women, to whom Flo was in the habit of passing out gold pieces, were impressed, while Billie Burke spent most of her married life attempting to elucidate his baffling complexities. It can only be concluded that Flo Ziegfeld deserves a prominent niche alongside Napoleon, Rasputin, Tallulah Bankhead, Mary Baker Eddy and other celebrated egomaniacs. It is probably fortunate for society as a whole that his prodigious energies were devoted to the relatively constructive efforts of Glorifying the American Girl. In any event, it is as the great showman of his age that he should and will be remembered.

Appendix

FOLLIES OF 1907 (Liberty Theatre, 8 July) featured Dave Lewis, Grace LaRue, Marion Sunshine, Prince Tokio, Mlle Dazie and Nora Bayes. *Music* by Seymour Firth, Vincent Bryan and others. *Book* by Harry B. Smith. *Designs* by W. H. Matthews, Jr. and Mme Freisinger. 70 Performances.

FOLLIES OF 1908 (New York Theatre, 15 June) featured Nora Bayes, Jack Norworth, Lucy Weston, Grace LaRue, William Powers, Mae Murray, George Bickel and Grace Leigh. *Book* by Harry B. Smith. *Music* by Maurice Levi, Jean Schwartz and Melville Gideon. *Costumes* by Edel of Paris, Mme Freisinger. *Sets* by John H. Young. 120 Performances.

FOLLIES OF 1909 (New York Theatre, 12 June) featured Nora Bayes, Jack Norworth, Lillian Lorraine, Mae Murray, Annabelle Whitford, Bessie Clayton and Arthur Deagon. *Book* by Harry B. Smith. *Music* by Levi and Gus Edwards. *Costumes and Sets* by Edel of Paris, W. H. Matthews, Jr. and John H. Young. 64 Performances.

FOLLIES OF 1910 (New York Theatre, 20 June) featured Fanny Brice, Bert Williams, Lillian Lorraine, Bobby North, Billie Reeves, Vera Maxwell and Anna Held (in film only). *Book* by Harry B. Smith. *Music* by Gus Edwards and others. *Sets and Costumes* by Young and Ernest Albert, Craig, Berlin, Tappé and W. H. Matthews Jr. 88 Performances.

FOLLIES OF 1911 (New York Theatre, 26 June) featured Bessie McCoy, Lillian Lorraine, Leon Errol, Fanny Brice, Bert Williams and the Dolly Sisters. *Music* by Levi, Raymond Hubbell, Jerome Kern and Irving Berlin. *Sets* by Albert and Unitt & Wickes. *Costumes* by W. H. Matthews Jr. and Tryce. 80 Performances.

FOLLIES OF 1912 (Moulin Rouge, 21 October) featured Elizabeth Brice, Leon Errol, Harry Watson, Jr., Bert Williams, Lillian Lorraine and Rae Samuels. *Book* by Harry B. Smith. *Costumes* by Schneider & Anderson. *Sets* by Ernest Albert. 88 Performances.

FOLLIES OF 1913 (New Amsterdam Theatre, 21 October) featured Leon Errol, Ann Pennington, Frank Tinney, Nat Wills and Elizabeth Brice. *Book* by Raymond Hubbell, Dave Stamper and Gene Buck. *Costumes* by Schneider & Anderson. *Sets* by Young and Anderson. 96 Performances.

FOLLIES OF 1914 (New Amsterdam, 1 July) featured Ed Wynn, Bert Williams, Ann Pennington, Kay Laurell, Leon Errol and Rita Gould. *Book* by Dave Stamper and Gene Buck. *Costumes* by Cora McGeachey & W. H. Matthews Jr. *Music* by a wide assortment of composers. 112 Performances.

FOLLIES OF 1915 (New Amsterdam, 16 June) featured W. C. Fields, Ed Wynn, Ina Claire, Ann Pennington, Bert Williams, Leon Errol, Mae Murray, George White, Kay Laurell, Justine Johnstone and Olive Thomas. *Book and Music* by Channing Pollock, Rennold Wolf, Dave Stamper and Gene Buck. *Costumes* by Lucile (Lady Duff-Gordon). *Sets* by Joseph Urban. 104 Performances.

FOLLIES OF 1916 (New Amsterdam, 12 June) featured Fanny Brice, Will Rogers, Bert Williams, W. C. Fields, Ann Pennington, Ina Claire, Marion Davies and Justine Johnstone. *Book* by Gene Buck and George V. Hobart. *Music* by Jerome Kern and Irving Berlin. *Costumes* by Lucile. *Sets* by Joseph Urban. 112 Performances.

FOLLIES OF 1917 (New Amsterdam, 12 June) featured Will Rogers, Eddie Cantor, W. C. Fields, Bert Williams, Fanny Brice, Lilyan Tashman, Dolores, Allyn King and Peggy Hopkins. *Book and Music* by Dave Stamper, Gene Buck and Victor Herbert. *Costumes* by Bendel and Lucile. *Sets* by Joseph Urban. 111 Performances.

FOLLIES OF 1918 (New Amsterdam, 18 June) featured Marilyn Miller, Will Rogers, Lillian Lorraine, Eddie Cantor, Frank Carter, W. C. Fields, Dolores, Kay Laurell, Savoy & Brennan and Joe Frisco. *Book* by Rennold Wolf and Gene Buck. *Music* by Jacobi, Louis Hirsch, Dave Stamper and Irving Berlin. *Costumes* by Lucile. Sets by Joseph Urban. 151 Performances.

FOLLIES OF 1919 (New Amsterdam, 23 June) featured Marilyn Miller, Eddie Cantor, Bert Williams, Eddie Dowling, Ray Dooley, Mary Hay and John Steel. *Book* by Gene Buck, Dave Stamper and Rennold Wolf. *Music* mainly by Irving Berlin and Victor Herbert. *Costumes* by Lucile and Mme Frances. *Sets* by Joseph Urban. 171 Performances.

FOLLIES OF 1920 (New Amsterdam, 22 June) featured Fanny Brice, W. C. Fields, Charles Winninger, Mary Eaton, Ray Dooley, John Steel and Jesse Reed. *Music* by Irving Berlin, Gene Buck and Victor Herbert. *Costumes* by Lucile. *Sets* by Joseph Urban. 123 Performances.

FOLLIES OF 1921 (Globe Theatre, 21 June) featured Fanny Brice, Raymond Hitchcock, W. C. Fields, Ray Dooley, Van & Schenck, Mary Eaton, Mary Lewis and John Clarke. *Book* by Willard Mack, Channing Pollock and others. *Music* by Jerome Kern, Rudolph Friml, Victor Herbert and B. G. DeSylva. *Costumes* by James Reynolds. *Sets* by Joseph Urban. 119 Performances.

FOLLIES OF 1922 (New Amsterdam, 5 June) featured Will Rogers, Gilda Gray, Evelyn Law, Mary Lewis, Mary Eaton, Gallagher & Shean and the Tiller Girls from London. *Book* by Ring Lardner, Ralph Spence and Gene Buck. *Music* by Victor Herbert, Dave Stamper and Louis Hirsch. *Costumes* by James Reynolds, Tappé and Charles Le Maire. *Sets* by Joseph Urban. A record run of 67 weeks in New York and 40 weeks on the road.

FOLLIES OF 1923 (New Amsterdam, 2 October) featured Fanny Brice, Ann Pennington, Lina Basquette, Imogene Wilson, Tom Lewis and Paul Whiteman's Orchestra. *Music* by Victor Herbert, Rudolph Friml, Dave Stamper and Gene Buck. *Costumes* by Erté of Paris, Tappé and James Reynolds. *Sets* by Joseph Urban. 333 Performances.

FOLLIES OF 1924 (New Amsterdam, 24 June) featured Will Rogers, Evelyn Law, Lupino Lane, Vivienne Segal and Ann Pennington. *Book* by Will Rogers and William A. McGuire. *Music* by Victor Herbert, Raymond Hubbell and others. *Costumes* by James Reynolds and Erté of Paris. *Sets* by Joseph Urban and John Wenger. Together with the following closely-linked edition, it ran for 402 performances.

FOLLIES OF 1925 (New Amsterdam, 6 July) featured W. C. Fields, Ray Dooley, the Tiller Girls, Peggy Fears and Al Oches. *Book* by W. C. Fields and J. P. McEvoy. *Costumes* by John Held Jr. and Ben Ali Haggin. *Sets* by Norman Bel Geddes. *Music* by Raymond Hubbell, Dave Stamper and Gene Buck.

FOLLIES OF 1927 (New Amsterdam, 16 August) featured Ruth Etting, Eddie Cantor, Claire Luce, Irene Delroy, The Albertina Rasch Girls and The Ingenues. *Book* by Harold Atteridge and Eddie Cantor. *Costumes* by John Harkrider. *Sets* by Joseph Urban. 167 Performances.

FOLLIES OF 1931 (Ziegfeld Theatre, 1 July) featured Harry Richman, Helen Morgan, Jack Pearl, Ruth Etting, Mitzi Mayfair, Hal Le Roy, Grace Moore and Gladys Glad. *Music and Sketches* by Gene Buck, Dave Stamper, Mark Hellinger, Harry Revel and Mack Gordon. *Costumes* by John Harkrider. *Sets* by Joseph Urban. 165 Performances.

Bibliography

Art And The Stage. Edited by Henning Rischbieter, Greenwich, Conn. N.Y. Graphic, 1968

Art Nouveau. Edited by Peter Selz and Mildred Constantine, Museum of Modern Art, New York, Doubleday, 1959

BARAL, Robert *Revue* New York: Fleet Publishing Corp. 1962

BRADY, William *Showman* New York: Dutton & Co. 1937

BURKE, Billie *With a Feather on My Nose* New York: Appleton-Century, Inc. 1949

CANTOR, Eddie *My Life is in Your Hands* New York: Harper 1928

CANTOR, Eddie *Take My Life* New York: Doubleday & Co. 1930

CANTOR, Eddie *Ziegfeld—The Great Glorifier* New York: A. King, 1934

CASTLE, Irene *Castles in the Air* New York: Doubleday & Co. 1958

CHURCHILL, Alan *Great White Way* New York: Dutton, 1962

CONRAD, Earl *Billy Rose; Manhatten Primitive* Cleveland: World Publishing, 1968

DAY, Donald *Will Rogers* New York: McKay, 1962

EWEN, David *Story of Irving Berlin* New York: Henry Holt & Co. 1950

EWEN, David *American Musical Theatre* New York: Henry Holt & Co. 1967

DUFF-GORDON, Lady Lucile *Discretions and Indiscretions* London: Jarrolds, 1932

FARNSWORTH, Marjorie *Ziegfeld Follies* New York: Putnam, 1956

FROHMAN, Daniel *Daniel Frohman Presents* New York: Lee Furman, 1937

HELD, Anna *Mémoires* Paris: La Nef de Paris, 1954

HIGHAM, Charles *Ziegfeld* Chicago: Henry Regnery & Co. 1973

KEATS, John *You Might as Well Live* New York: Simon & Schuster, 1970

KOBAL, John *Pictorial History of Film Musicals* New York-London: 1972

173

MORRIS, Lloyd *Incredible New York* New York: Random House, 1951

NATHAN, George *The Theatre, The Drama, The Girls* New York: Knopf, 1921

ROGERS, Will *Autobiography* Boston: Houghton Mifflin, 1949

SOBEL, Bernard *Broadway Heartbeat* New York: Hermitage House

SOBEL, Louis *The Longest Street* New York: Crown, 1968

SPENCER, Charles *Erté* New York: C. N. Potter, 1970. London: Studio Vista, 1970

STAGG, Jerry *The Brothers Shubert* New York: Random House, 1968

SWANBERG, W. A. *Citizen Hearst* New York: Charles Scribner, 1961

Theatre Art. Edited by Simonson, Lee, New York: Cooper Square-Museum Modern Art, 1934

TURKUS, BURTON & FEDER, Sid *Murder, Inc.* New York: Farrar & Straus, 1951

URBAN, Joseph *Theatres* Boston: Theatre Arts, 1927

WODEHOUSE & BOLTON *Bring on The Girls* New York: Simon & Schuster, 1953

ZIEGFELD, Patricia *The Ziegfelds' Girl* Boston: Little Brown, 1964

Index

175

176